voices in the
wilderness

ISBN 978-1886591-2-33

Manufactured in the United States of America

Published in cooperation with
Blue Creek Press
Box 110 • Heron, Montana • 59844
www.bluecreekpress.com
books@bluecreekpress.com

CINNABAR

FOUNDATION

www.thecinnabarfoundation.org

This book is a joint project of
Montana Wilderness Association and
Friends of Scotchman Peaks Wilderness
with assistance from the Cinnabar Foundation and the High Stakes Foundation

The voices contained herein are from
in and around the Kootenai National
Forest, in Sanders and Lincoln Counties,
Montana. We thank *The Western News*
of Libby and *The Sanders County Ledger*
of Thompson Fall for their help with this
effort.

MONTANA WILDERNESS
ASSOCIATION
www.wildmontana.org

FRIENDS OF
SCOTCHMAN PEAKS
Since 2005
Working for WILDERNESS
www.scotchmanpeaks.org

HIGH STAKES
foundation

INCREASING THE ODDS FOR EVERYONE
https://highstakesfoundation
.wordpress.com

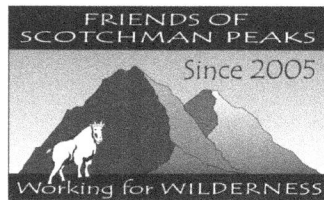

voices
in the
wilderness

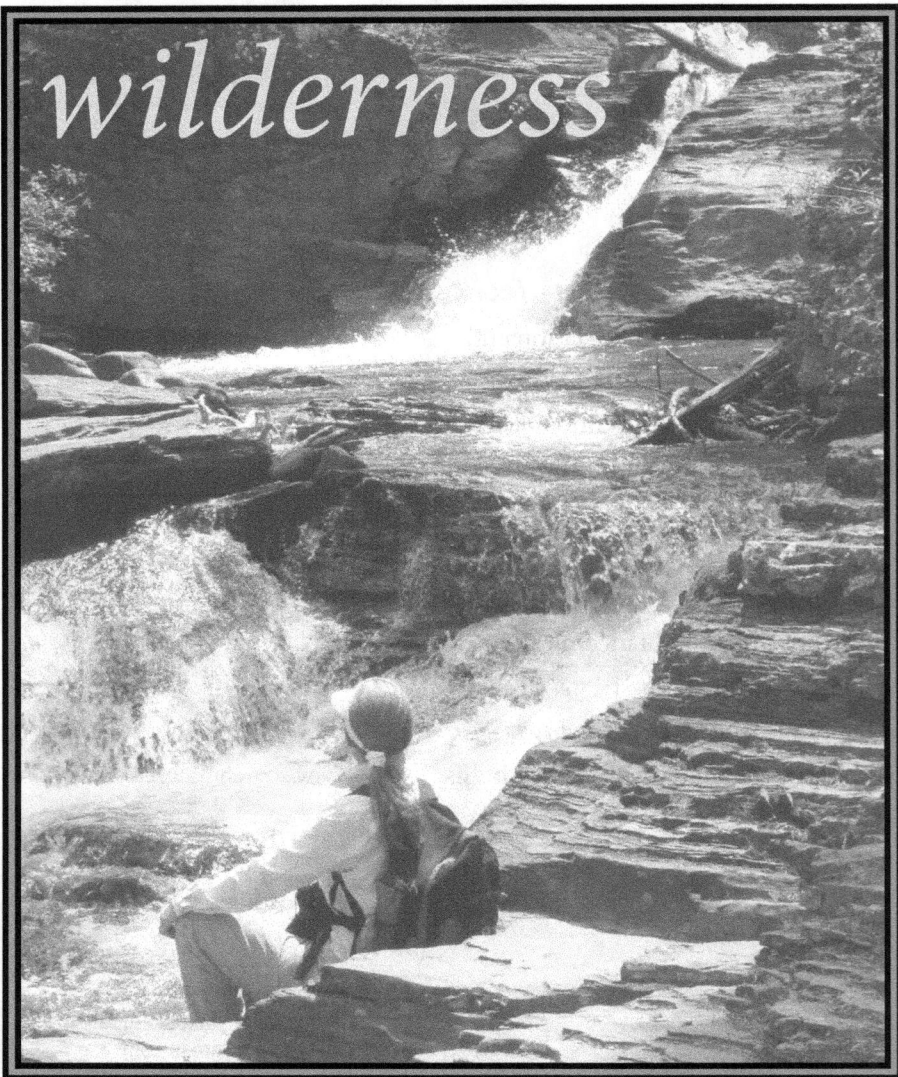

a collection of wild essays

Friends of Scotchman Peaks Wilderness • Montana Wilderness Association

where we come from

In the Kootenai National Forest of northwest Montana the pace of life may seem slower than in other places. We rise with the sun on the mountains, match the flow of the rivers and slow down at sunset. We are connected to the land. We work, we hunt, we fish, we hike, we paddle and play out of doors. We live close to wilderness, with and without a capital "W."

If and when we leave, we take parts of the Cabinet Mountains Wilderness, the Yaak Valley, Scotchman Peaks, and the Kootenai and Clark Fork rivers with us, but we also leave parts of ourselves with them. When we come back, we find ourselves whole again.

As Gene Reckin writes in his essay on page 13: "Humans need a place to cleanse the heart, the mind and the soul, and to re-connect with the land, the air, and the water that nourishes us. Whether it be an untrammeled coastline, a red desert gorge, an alpine meadow, or a mountain top, that place is called wilderness. I chose to raise my children in Kootenai Country and the Cabinet Mountains, so that they might be nurtured like I was, surrounded by family, friends, and wild places."

Voices in the Wilderness is a collection of authentic northwestern Montana voices who love and live parts of their lives in wild country. In their stories, we find the value of the untamed places that surround us.

For these voices and for the many others who have things to say about their love of wilderness, we work to keep the wild world wild.

where we are

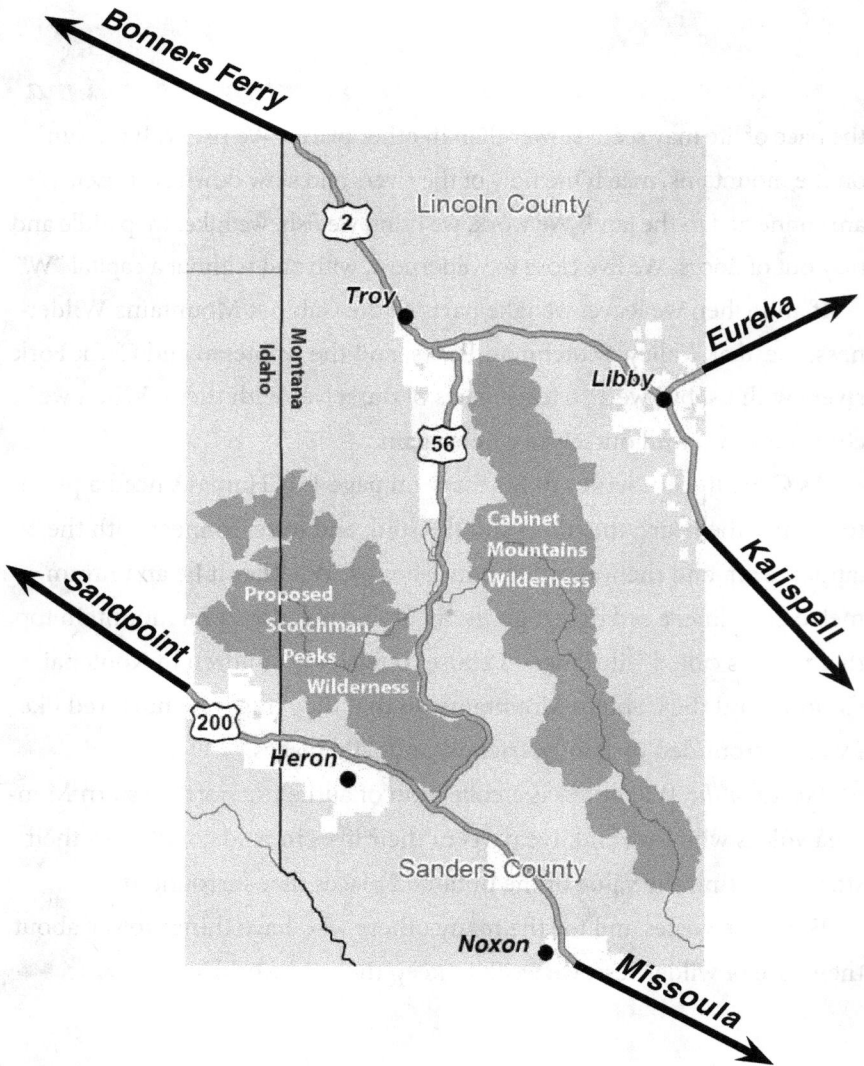

Bonners Ferry

Lincoln County

2

Troy

Idaho

Montana

Eureka

Libby

56

Cabinet
Mountains
Wilderness

Sandpoint

Proposed
Scotchman
Peaks
Wilderness

Kalispell

200

Heron

Sanders County

Noxon

Missoula

The Scotchman Peaks
recommended wilderness

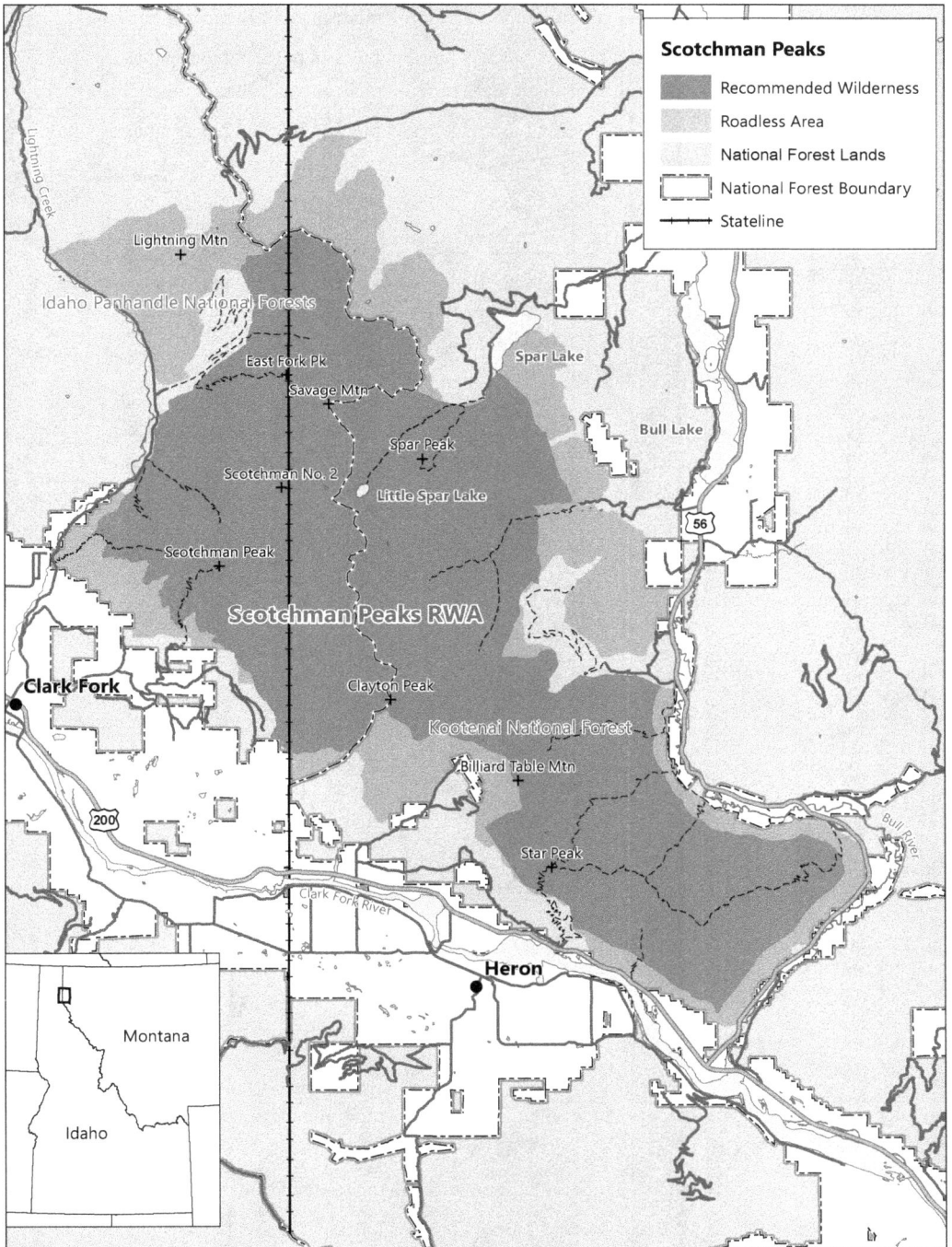

Scotchman Peaks

- Recommended Wilderness
- Roadless Area
- National Forest Lands
- National Forest Boundary
- Stateline

Lightning Creek

Lightning Mtn

Idaho Panhandle National Forests

Spar Lake

East Fork Pk

Savage Mtn

Bull Lake

Spar Peak

Scotchman No. 2

Little Spar Lake

56

Scotchman Peak

Scotchman Peaks RWA

Clark Fork

Clayton Peak

Kootenai National Forest

Billiard Table Mtn

200

Star Peak

Clark Fork River

Bull River

Heron

Montana

Idaho

Cabinet Mountains Wilderness
north half

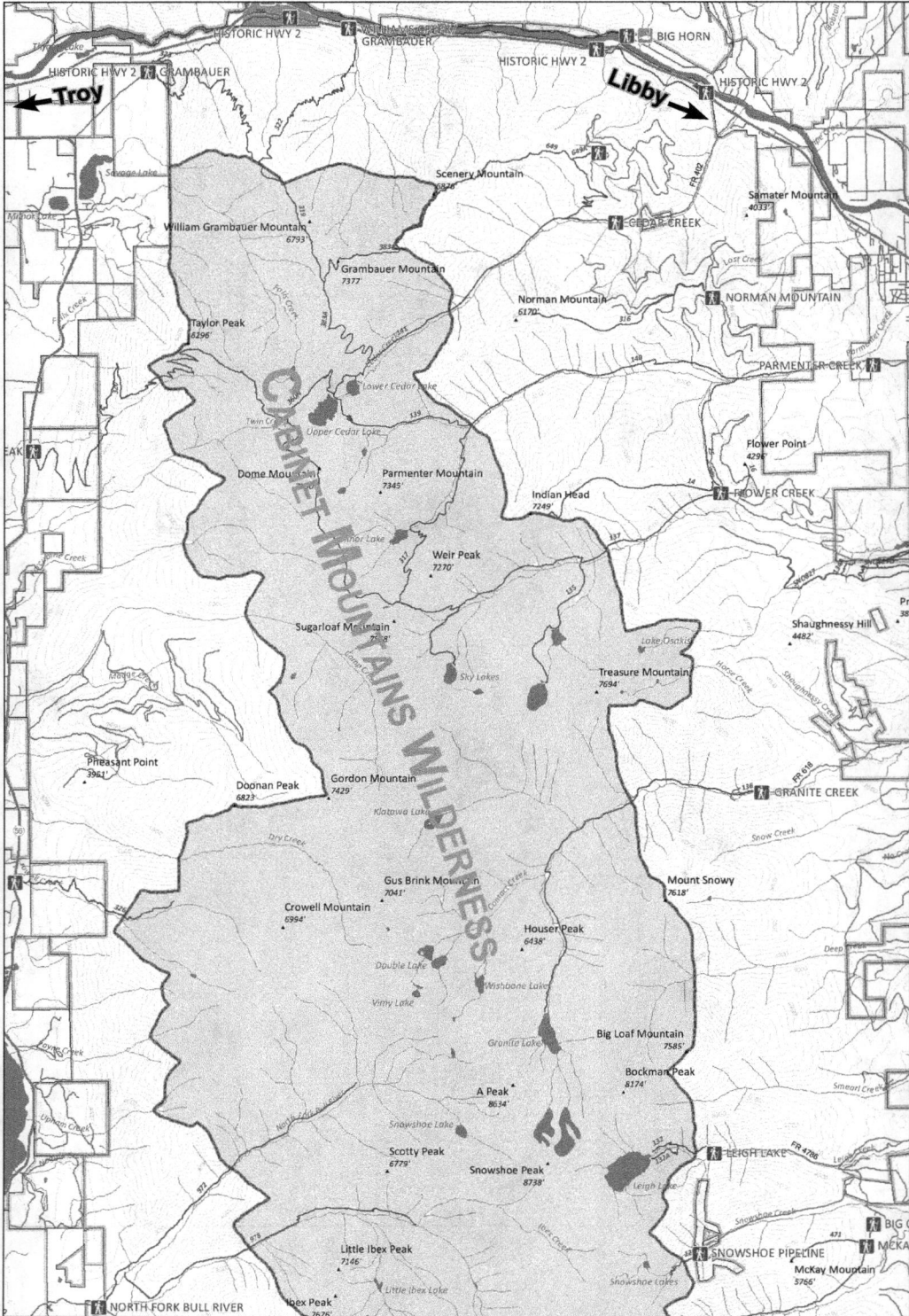

← Troy

Libby →

HISTORIC HWY 2
WILLIAM GREW GRAMBAUER
BIG HORN
HISTORIC HWY 2
GRAMBAUER
HISTORIC HWY 2

Savage Lake

Minor Lake

Scenery Mountain
6876'

CEDAR CREEK

Samater Mountain
4033'

William Grambauer Mountain
6793'

Fish Creek

Grambauer Mountain
7377'

Norman Mountain
6170'

NORMAN MOUNTAIN

Lost Creek

Taylor Peak
6296'

Kale Creek

PARMENTER CREEK

Lower Cedar Lake

Upper Cedar Lake

Twin Creek

Dome Mountain

Parmenter Mountain
7345'

Indian Head
7249'

Flower Point
4296'

FLOWER CREEK

Arbor Lake

Weir Peak
7270'

Sugarloaf Mountain

Lake Osakis

Shaughnessy Hill
4482'

Sky Lakes

Treasure Mountain
7694'

Horse Creek

Moose Creek

Pheasant Point
3961'

Doonan Peak
6823'

Gordon Mountain
7429'

Klatawa Lake

Dry Creek

GRANITE CREEK

Snow Creek

Gus Brink Mountain
7041'

Crowell Mountain
6994'

Mount Snowy
7618'

Houser Peak
6438'

Double Lake

Wishbone Lake

Vimy Lake

Deep Creek

Granite Lake

Big Loaf Mountain
7585'

Bockman Peak
8174'

Smeorl Creek

A Peak
8634'

Snowshoe Lake

North Fork Bull River

Scotty Peak
6779'

Snowshoe Peak
8738'

Leigh Lake

LEIGH LAKE

Upham Creek

Little Ibex Peak
7146'

Little Ibex Lake

SNOWSHOE PIPELINE

McKay Mountain
3766'

Ibex Peak
7676'

Snowshoe Lakes

NORTH FORK BULL RIVER

Cabinet Mountains Wilderness
south half

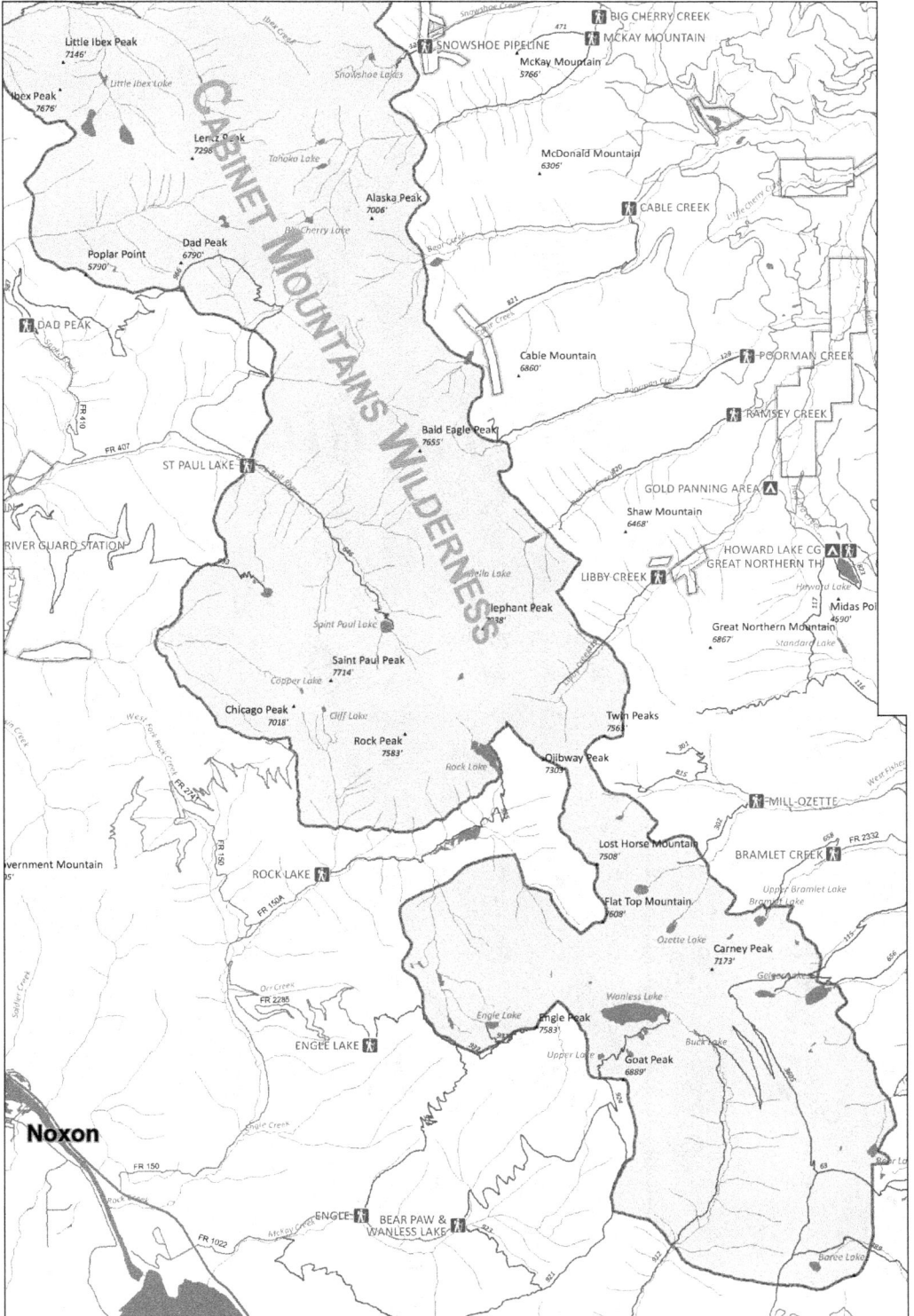

Little Ibex Peak
7146'

Little Ibex Lake

Ibex Peak
7676'

Ibex Creek

Lenz Peak
7298'

Tahoka Lake

CABINET MOUNTAINS WILDERNESS

Snowshoe Creek

471

SNOWSHOE PIPELINE

BIG CHERRY CREEK

MCKAY MOUNTAIN

Snowshoe Lakes

McKay Mountain
5766'

McDonald Mountain
6306'

Alaska Peak
7006'

Big Cherry Lake

CABLE CREEK

Little Cherry Cr

Dad Peak
6790'

Poplar Point
5790'

Red Creek

821

DAD PEAK

FR 410

FR 407

Cable Mountain
6860'

POORMAN CREEK

Poorman Creek

RAMSEY CREEK

128

Big Creek

Bald Eagle Peak
7655'

ST PAUL LAKE

St Paul Cr

820

GOLD PANNING AREA

RIVER GUARD STATION

Shaw Mountain
6468'

HOWARD LAKE CG
GREAT NORTHERN TH

Isabella Lake

LIBBY CREEK

Howard Lake

Spint Paul Lake

Elephant Peak
7038'

Midas Pol
4590'

Great Northern Mountain
6867'

Standard Lake

Saint Paul Peak
7714'

Copper Lake

West Fork Rock Creek

Chicago Peak
7018'

Cliff Lake

Twin Peaks
7563'

Rock Peak
7583'

Rock Lake

Ojibway Peak
7309'

FR 271

FR 150

Government Mountain

ROCK LAKE

FR 150A

Lost Horse Mountain
7508'

MILL-OZETTE

BRAMLET CREEK

FR 2332

Upper Bramlet Lake
Bramlet Lake

Flat Top Mountain
7608'

Ozette Lake

Carney Peak
7173'

Orr Creek

FR 2285

Wanless Lake

Engle Lake

Engle Peak
7583'

Buck Lake

ENGLE LAKE

Upper Lake

Goat Peak
6889'

Noxon

Engle Creek

FR 150

ENGLE

BEAR PAW &
WANLESS LAKE

FR 1022

McKay Creek

Baree Lake

voices in the
wilderness

table of contents

voices in the wilderness

getting lost:
an introduction

***Not until we are lost do we begin to understand ourselves.* — Thoreau.**

"You look lost."

It's the first thing a friend says as I walk into the noisy mélange of a July lakefront restaurant. The deck is full of folk I know and don't know being served by a staff I was once part of. A familiar band plays to the lake beyond the crowd. It's 7:20 and I traversed out of the East Fork at noon, where I have for a few nights and days been not lost, even when I was over my head in tag alder, devil's club, blowdown and rock. Put me on an elk trail and let me choose where I want to go. I am not lost. Put me in the midst of this. I am lost.

But not permanently, though I should have learned by now to break myself back into "civilization" more gently that this. I am capable of coming back to this world. I've done it many times, albeit sometimes — nay, often — reluctantly, unwillingly. All of this hyperactivity and noise and illusory social gaiety can't match the moments of solitary route finding in the East Fork, perhaps because the latter is so rare and the former seem so mundane and repetitious.

Yesterday, Saturday afternoon; we are in the jungle
and I am seeking an elk tread to follow on toward "home," a camp in the East Fork Meadow. One of my fellows finds a clew and we puzzle it out to arrive at our chosen destination. I am reminded of a moment four years ago when I set this self-same young man out front and he took the lead, learning to think like an elk. I was proud that day to be with him, and I'm proud this day to be part of that foundation that allows him to find his way and ours. I am pleased to know we are not only not lost, but will not be, as long as we know where we want to be next.

By tenacity and endeavor, we will arrive.

There should be something new to write about this place, but there is not. Nothing here is new. All is ancient. The mosquitoes and huckleberries are the newest individual arrivals, but they have been here all along, ever since the ice finished with the place and before.

Yet I learn something new each time I come here; a new bit of trail, a small, yet lovely fresh vista, a new way to almost get where I want to go before I have to resort to whacking bushes and cursing tag alder. In the heat of those sorts of wanderings, I wonder why I bother, but I know why. Each lesson is a precious piece of a colossal puzzle I will never solve. But, it isn't the puzzle of the place that I come here to resolve, but my own self. Resolution. Renewal. Reasons to keep on keeping on. Recreation.

voices in the
wilderness

We misunderstand that last word, equate it with "fun," "entertainment," even "self-indulgence." We make a thoughtless act of it — or something we can buy — and place it beside our wants, like movies and television and McDonalds. It is more sacred than those. And not so easy. Re-creation is not something we do or pay for, but something that happens to us when we let go. When we surrender to wilderness — wild places physical, spiritual, mental — we are recreated, torn down to our foundations and rebuilt anew in our own best image.

There is not a better place to get lost, I don't think, than in wilderness, capital W or no. When the life you thought you knew so well becomes discombooberated by confusion over which way is home, a lot of that life also becomes somewhat superficial and unimportant. It's hard to apply any significance to the 42-inch plasma screen when you are distracted by the thought that you have no idea of where you are or how you got there.

It's happened to me. Several times, in fact. It may happen again. In fact, I hope it does — sort of. Getting lost implies that one is taking chances, visiting new places, pushing boundaries. Getting lost might also mean that you are, of your own volition, removing yourself from the familiar, the comfortable, the well known. This is an exercise in independence, I think, and can lead to some very interesting lessons about who you are and how you handle yourself in both slight and dire emergencies.

Wild places are easy to get lost in, if only temporarily. No sidewalks, no fences, no man-made trails, no you-are-here signs. It's just you and the planet and those next few steps. I've been lost in tag alder patches for a few minutes and on steep sidehills for a few hours. And, I've been lost in the wilderness for days on end; not really lost in the sense that I don't know where I am or how to get home, but lost to the frantic, crazy world of the internet, pavement and paychecks.

getting lost:
an introduction

Tonight, I am not so sure that this sun-soaked deck
and its denizens can be deemed "civilized." As vague and tentative as elk
trails can be, the social trails here are even more so. At least they are for me.

It is the wilderness that draws me in and then draws me out, shows me
who I am. And it is up to me to remember what it shows me: to just be
and avoid thinking too much, which can lead to drinking too much and
other social dilemmas.

Home. Dishes. Laundry. Monday morning looms on the horizon like
a forest fire in need of fighting. "Let it burn!" says the wild part of me, the
wilderness part that knows 100 years is like a single, solitary heartbeat to
the planet.

How good it is to know that one single, solitary lesson learned in a
place that tells us nothing new, but knows all the oldies: peace, persever-
ance, patience; solitude, silence, sacredness. Presence without pretense;
being, untied from doing; seeing. untied from wanting; living, untied
from waiting. Forward. One step at a time. Rest. Until it seems time to
stand. Look! For new hidden in the ancient.

"Learn," the wilderness says. "Learn! Open your eyes, your ears, your
nostrils, your pores, your heart and learn. Who. You. Are."

"You are not lost."

o————————o

A number of "voices in the wilderness" follow,
tales about time well-spent being "lost" in wilderness. I hope you will
find some to stir your heart and motivate you to get lost yourself. It is my
further hope that you will recognize the value of wild places and enlist
as part of the nationwide community of people who are "working for
wilderness."

— *Sandy Compton*
editor, voices in the wilderness

Kelly Palmer is a former fishing guide and outfitter and the counselor at Troy High School. He and his wife have raised four children under the Big Sky, and now live in Troy where she is the 7-12 grade art teacher and he has been the school counselor for the past 19 years.

time to go — go fishing

I've had the privilege of living in a drift boat on the
Kootenai River for seventeen summers. I've spent 550-575 days guiding fishermen--some of whom have become good friends, others who are fond memories and a small handful who need to expire so I can write the book.

I've come to realize you can have too much of a good thing. Guiding is like having chocolate cake every day for dessert--it can be awesome cake, but it gets old day after day. I needed a change.

I found myself looking to the mountains more often and realizing that I'd spent very little time "up there." Combined with the realization that I wasn't getting any younger and the "chocolate cake every day" syndrome, it proved to be the mystical amalgamation of elements required to pull the backpacking gear out of the garage where it has been resting for too many years.

To borrow from John Muir, the mountains were calling, and it was time for me to go. Go fishing, that is.

voices in the
wilderness

My bride was worried. I left my National Forest map with her with my route highlighted. I knew where I was going, and had my Garmin eTrex with me. While the GPS is pretty handy in the field, it's not as good for the bigger picture. I knew I was looking for Forest Service road 455 (not the real number). What I didn't know is that there is more than one Forest Service road 455.

I'll tell you — 455D is not the one you want. It dead-ends in some guy's driveway. Thankfully, he wasn't the shootin' type. When I explained what I was doing, he looked at me with concern and asked if I wanted to call my wife.

"Why?" I asked.

"Well, you know, so she knows where you were last seen in case they need to find your remains."

I kid you not — that's what he said.

"No, I think I'm good," I replied. He gave me another map that made it easy to find the correct version of that elusive road 455.

Forty-five minutes later, I parked the truck. I found the thinnest spot in the dog-hair tangle alder and initiated the hardest hike of my life.

My parking spot was at 4391 feet. I would crest the ridge almost exactly one mile later at 7120 feet. That's right: the slope averaged more than 45 degrees.

It took me five hours.

Initially, the landscape was dominated by western red cedar, hemlock, devil's club and ferns. After a bit, lodgepole pine interspersed with huckleberries and other shrubs prevailed. Eventually, alpine fir and rock defined the hillside.

My "hike" wound up with a fair amount of mountaineering to it. On the ridge I was only 400 yards from the lake. However, it was 800 vertical feet below me. My legs were unsteady. My pack had doubled in weight. With no water, I couldn't stay on the ridge and I couldn't go back. Against my best judgment, I headed down toward the lake.

Slowly.

A hard hour later I arrived.

It's an amazing sensation to be alone in the wilderness. I become keenly aware that an inconvenience in town--sprained ankle, forgotten rain coat, no pocketknife--can be a life-threatening problem in the wild. I realize that I am smaller in the grand scheme of things than I generally acknowledge, and being at the top of the food chain is an artificial construct.

I made camp. The weather was simply perfect. I enjoyed a meal of dehydrated kung pow chicken washed down with Gatorade and five ibuprofen for dessert. Sleep came easily and uninterrupted.

The next morning I enjoyed a breakfast of hot granola with blueberries and military surplus Irish cream coffee surrogate and five more ibuprofen.

After breakfast, I strung up my fly rod. There were sporadic rises, although I couldn't see what they were eating. I'd seen grasshoppers and yellow jackets around camp, so I tried patterns to match. No luck.

Plan B was a simple olive marabou leech. Twenty minutes later I held a living example of perfection.

I stood awestruck at the beauty of the first golden trout I've ever touched. I snapped a quick photo and slipped her back into the water. It sounds simple, and it is: I was completely happy in that moment.

I find comfort in the solitude and beauty of the high places. When there, my thoughts wander to everything and nothing, all at once. Life is put in perspective, and I am at peace.

voices in the
wilderness

Jon Jeresek is a retired USFS employee. After nearly 40 years with the Agency, including time as a fire fighter and timber beast, his fondest memories are the relationships he enjoyed with wilderness rangers, trail crews, and avalanche forecasters.

Jon
Jeresek

a natural history: fire and ice in the cabinets

The East Cabinet Range that makes up the Cabinet
Mountains Wilderness is ancient beyond comprehension. The Belt
Formation composed of metamorphosed sediments dates back to the pre
Cambrian geologic period, over a billion years! This Formation with its
gentle folds and faults that trend from southeast to northwest has been
sculpted by successive continental ice sheets and alpine glaciers: The
most recent ended 10,000 years ago.

Wilderness as an idea and more recently as a designation of land, oc-
cupies only a nano-second in the life of these mountains. Consider the
minds of Carhart and Leopold who early in the development of western
civilization could forsee the need for wild places for a multitude of social
values. Consider the efforts of Marshall and Zahniser to establish such

areas for the benefit of all people. And finally on September 3, 1964, the
Wilderness Act becomes the law of our land. How insignificant we are
in the passage of time. And yet, our individual personal goal in life is
to make a difference! We would have better luck if we were an insect, a
fungus, a spark of fire, or even a snowflake.

In our brief time on the landscape of these mountains as natives or as
European settlers, we have seen change that does not go unnoticed. Some
change occurs with the passage of time (evolution) while other change
comes at the hand of man. With 1964 as a starting point, let us consider
what changes are easily observable.

From the late 1950s to the mid 1960s, a native small
tan moth and its hungry off spring (Choristoneura occidentalis), known
as western spruce budworm, are finishing dinner. Nearly five million
acres of Engellman spuce have been repeatedly defoliated in the Northern
Rockies causing mortality, especially in mature trees. Response to this
widespread natural infestation is harvesting of dead and at risk stands
of old growth spruce largely at upper elevations. By 1964, the Cabinet
Mountains Wilderness boundary has in many locations been determined
by the pattern of spruce harvest. Spruce stumps of legendary size are still
seen in the headwaters of Ramsey, Poorman, and Bear Creeks.

The hand of man sets the stage for this next agent of change in the
Cabinet Mountains Wilderness. In the early 1900s a shipment of white
pine seedlings from Europe arrives in Vancouver BC. It carries a complex
micro organism, the fungus Cronartium ribicola, aka white pine blister rust. There are no inspectors; the shipment is not impounded. The
seedlings are sold and distributed. Initially, life for this fungus is not easy.
It requires two different host plants to complete its life cycle. By 1921,
the fungus establishes itself on mountain gooseberry or currant (Ribes

spp) bushes around Vancouver. Then fungal spores are transported by the wind from the Ribes leaves to any white pine species. Entry into the pine is through needle openings where the fungus grows slowly into the woody twig. The infected branch will swell and the bark will blister revealing the bright orange fungal spores. Disease progression is usually slow and can take years to reach the mainstem where top kill then becomes evident.

By 1927, the fungus is observed on white pine in northwestern Montana. Once this complicated life cycle was discovered forest managers sought to eliminate the Ribes host plant thereby interrupting the fungus life cycle. Protection of high value western white pine stands motivated managers. Large scale Ribes eradication programs were conducted for years by the Civilian Conservation Corps to no avail. Through time, wind transported spores found whitebark pine at higher elevations and disease progression opened a new chapter. Most high elevation ridges in the Cabinets exhibit silver snags of long dead whitebark pines. The disease successfully attacks all ages of whitebark pine. Natural resistance to this disease has been found in isolated pockets, example Cabinet Divide above Baree Lake. Here cones are protected from nutcrackers and squirrels, then harvested and sent to nurseries for plantings.

Mother nature exhibits her most fickle behavior
through the snow she blankets the Cabinet Range with each year. From the last ice age forward, winter weather has responded to the ocean temperatures as driven by the sun. Most recently we talk about El Nino and La Nina cycles and the influence man's activities have on them. Rather than think in generalities, let's think about the year 2014. It is the 50th anniversary of the passage of the Wilderness Act. However, it is a most special year for snow in the Cabinets. No, it is not the year with the most

snow, but it is the year with the most snow movement since 1964. Snow and its movement are possibly the greatest influence on vegetation spatially within the Wilderness.

Let's look at the benchmark events. Late October 2013, the first lasting snows cover the upper elevations. On November 19, a rain on snow event creates a 3-4 inch thick knife hard crust that is bomb proof. December and early January are pretty normal for snowfall. January 11, a wind event is so strong that snow "tornados" are reported. This wind also transports "pink" clay from the Palouse to give the snowpack in Lincoln County a rosy hue. First week of February is snowless, calm and bitterly cold. Temperatures rarely get above 0'F during the daytime. It is getting very interesting! We now have a rock solid base layer with deep surface hoar overlaying it. It starts snowing and snowing and *snowing*.

February 11, avalanche risk rises dramatically with massive storm loading and wind transport. By February 14 we have widespread snowpack instability and the Avalanche Center issues a *high* hazard advisory for the entire forecast area (E.Cabinets, W.Cabinets, Purcells). By February 22, we are investigating six human burials and a fatality. People are triggering slides remotely, ie. they are in a low slope zone when they trigger snowpack collapse that propagates uphill to a starting zone that then releases upon them! High hazard conditions persist for nearly a month. Then on March 6, the mother of all snow movement events occurs! A prolonged rain on snow event triggers hard slab releases on 60% of all north aspect chutes in the Cabinets and 40% of the south aspect chutes. Trees several hundred years old are uprooted or broken off to be carried down slope. Hard snow scours the ground dislodging rocks, brush and smaller trees. The widening of existing chutes and creation of new ones is hard to phathom. 2014 summer trail work reveals newly created avalanche chutes across trails in Cedar Creek, S.Fk Parmenter Creek, Flower Creek, Granite Creek, and Leigh Creek.

Lightning and resulting fires are the most politicized and polarizing agents of change in Wilderness. In 1910, nearly all of northwest Montana was "wilderness." On August 20-21 of that fateful year, a low level jet stream wind with sustained speeds near 60 mph picked up numerous small debris burning fires and pushed them northeasterly into a massive flame front. In those two days, nearly 3 million acres were scorched and over 87 lives were lost. Understandably, that event was the birthdate for modern fire suppression in the Forest Service. Suppression would evolve to use every resource and technological advantage possible to suppress fires as soon after detection as possible. Through decades of experience and study of fire, modern land managers have come to appreciate the benefits and necessity of fire on the landscape. This change has not come easily.

Since 1964, within the Cabinet Mountains Wilderness, fire has been a sporadic agent of change. To be significant, fire must have perfect timing of several events. First, normal drying of Wilderness fuels occurs after August 10th. Then a significant lightning event must pass over wilderness elevations. And finally, a significant wind event must have access to a fire start. This happens rarely within the Cabinet Mountains. In 1967, the Sky Fire covered several thousand acres and was aggressively suppressed from the start. Hand fire lines and fuel breaks are still visible today on Google Earth images. In 1994, a benchmark year for fire on the Kootenai, over 200 fires we ignited by the August 14th lightning storm. Due to the number of fires and limited resources, fires in the wilderness were initially monitored only. Then as resources became available, suppression actions were taken on a few fires (Hanging Flower, Leigh, McKay) that posed a risk if a significant fire run were to occur.

1994 saw 20 fires in wilderness cover nearly 9,000 acres largely for lack of suppression resources. By contrast, 1998 saw 19 wilderness fires that were suppressed from their start. The Dome Fire sat dormant near Upper Cedar Lake for 10 days before winds on September 2-3 pushed it 3,340 acres. The other 18 wilderness fires that year only covered 6.2 acres. August 10, 2000, brought lightning fires to the extreme ends of the 34 mile long East Cabinet Range. Here 16 fires covered over 2,500 acres around Taylor Peak, Grambauer Mountain, Falls Creek, Green Mountain, and Engle Peak. Fire fighting resources were available and used to suppress these fires.

2015 ushered in a new Forest Management Plan that included enlightened policy to deal with natural ignitions (lightning). Monitoring, confinement and containment strategies were now available to wilderness managers. Fire could now be allowed to play its natural ecological role in the Cabinets and elsewhere. On August 14th, a lightning storm passed over the Cabinets igniting several fires in the southern half of the wilderness. Some fires were monitored, some had confinement strategies implemented, but very few had direct suppression activities. The Klatawa Fire of nearly 5,000 acres had no direct suppression activities until October 21. Then a predicted cold front passage spurred the construction of a hand fuel break and fireline at the northeast fire edge. The cold front bypassed the Klatawa Fire.

For now, man-caused fires in wilderness (average 2/yr) will be suppressed. Natural ignitions will be monitored, confined, contained, or suppressed. Through our age of enlightenment concerning the place of fire in ecosystems, possibly man's use of fire will become a tool to achieve wilderness benefits. Alas, fire is as natural in the wilderness as insects, disease, snow, and wind.

Blackwell Glacier from Snowshoe Peak
in the Cabinet Mountains Wilderness

voices in the
wilderness

Gene Reckin was born in 1954 and raised in San Diego, California, while also spending many life-changing summers in Yosemite National Park. Gene taught science in Libby Public Schools for 34 years, and spends as much of his "spare time" as possible exploring the west in a canoe or in his hiking boots, bird watching, building furniture, hunting, and gardening.

a "wild" childhood led me here

I was 5 years old in June of 1959 when my father took a summer job as a seasonal ranger in the high country of Yosemite National Park. I remember shedding tears of resistance about this unknown adventure, as it would require me to leave my friends and our games of kickball in the streets of San Diego among other forms of play that youngsters create in the "urban jungle." But it was off to the unfamiliar, and it would change my life forever.

Our '52 Chevy, loaded with the bare necessities of gear to last us all summer, labored through the night as we headed north, avoiding the heat of the Mojave Desert and skirting the east slope of the grand Sierra Nevada, arriving at the base of Lee Vining canyon at dawn. Our ascension to the park entrance at Tioga Pass with the rising sun at our backs was an extraordinary sensory and emotional experience, and one my family would repeat many times through my childhood. It became a pilgrimage of sorts, and the eight summers we spent in the wilderness setting of Yosemite's high country, free from the distractions and complications of life in the big city, were the best times my family spent together.

*I have always been curious about what kinds of de-*tails a person stores in long-term memory and why other things quickly leave us. As I look back on my most vivid memories of those childhood adventures, many are indeed sensory. My inexperienced senses had been overwhelmed and consequently dulled by a constant barrage of the rank smell of automobile exhaust, the glare of city lights, and the dull roar of noise punctuated by car horns, sirens, and jet engines overhead. Lee Vining canyon introduced me to the sweet smell of high desert sage, the alpine meadows of Yosemite were home to the aroma of wild onion and a myriad of wildflower species, and to this day I still stick my nose into the furrowed bark of Jeffery and Ponderosa Pine, the "vanilla trees" as we called them.

I had no idea how blue a sky could be, nor how many stars were being hidden by the brown blanket of smog over my home town. Yet a moonless night on Tioga Pass at ten thousand feet revealed an incredible display of the heavens, my first hint that we on earth may not be alone in the universe. And the quiet uncovered the songs of the Stellars Jays, the Clark's Nutcrackers, and the Mountain Chickadees. There was a new, soothing roar in the background; the sound of water cascading over rocks, the wind blowing through the trees, and often there was absolutely no sound at all. Perhaps the most enjoyable treat of all was to lay on my belly at the edge of a stream and drink the clear, fresh water that was so cold that it almost hurt my teeth. Yes, indeed, it was a whole new world.

But that world is becoming increasingly crowded. I was fortunate to be able to experience Yosemite in the last of the 'good old days'. Since that time the population of our country has doubled and the population of California has almost tripled. The world population increases by about 220,000 people every day. That's about a 'Spokanes-worth' of people - every day. The pressures placed on all of our resources are mounting quickly. Visionaries like John Muir and Theodore Roosevelt were inspired by the beauty and wildness of places like Yosemite and understood the urgency to preserve such places for generations to come. My family, and millions upon millions of others, are certainly the beneficiaries of their foresight. As a teacher of biology, I now understand the many values of wilderness beyond the personal and experiential, but those times of youthful exploration and growth, in wild places all over the west, have shaped the person that I am today.

Humans need a place to cleanse the heart, the mind and the soul, and to re-connect with the land, the air, and the water that nourish us. Whether it be an untrammeled coastline, a red desert gorge, an alpine meadow, or a mountain top, that place is called wilderness. I chose to raise my children in Kootenai Country and the Cabinet Mountains, so that they might be nurtured like I was, surrounded by family, friends, and wild places.

In the words of President Lyndon Johnson upon signing the Wilderness Act of 1964, "If future generations are to remember us with gratitude rather than contempt, we must leave them more than the miracles of technology. We must leave them a glimpse of the world as it was in the beginning, not just after we got through with it."

voices in the
wilderness

Anthony South grew up in bustling Bellevue, Washington, polar opposite of the place he has grown to love.

He moved to Troy, Montana in his freshman year of high school and instantly became fascinated with the thing called Wilderness. From that moment on, he has been "out there" hiking, camping, & doing whatever it takes to make that possible.

Anthony lives in the Yaak River valley with his wife Ashley. He works for the Yaak Valley Forest Council.

necessity

On a cold, early-July morning at a high mountain lake sheltered beneath a towering summit, Westslope cutthroat start rising, breaking the crystal clear glass surface. Well over half the lake is bordered by a basin walled with cliffs and crags rising to the peak that I have gazed longingly at for years. The other portion of the lake is lined with twisted, ancient old growth forest. This is where I choose to be.

Yesterday, I woke up with a smile, got myself — and my pack — ready in record time, and set out for the hour-long drive to the trailhead that would lead me to the scenic beauty of the Cabinet Mountain Wilderness. There is something about the first few steps on the trail; they are full of anticipation, stiff muscles, joints not quite getting into the rhythm they will be going through for hours, and happiness — always happiness. Four and a half hours later I arrive at my destination, a high mountain basin where snow-fed waters created a liquid jewel. I quickly set up camp, trying to beat the darkness, and boil some water to bring my dehydrated Katmandu Curry and Rice to life. I effortlessly fall asleep.

In the morning I reluctantly crawl out of my sleeping bag and throw on as many layers as possible. It may be summer to everyone else, but it sure doesn't feel like it here. There is a glittery blanket of frost over everything. It reminded me of phrase from a short story I read once that summarized alpine climbing and mountaineering. "If you are not hungry, you are carrying too much food; if you are warm, you have too many clothes. . . ." In some strange way, this made me feel better because I apparently didn't bring too many clothes or too much food. I was still cold and my infant size bowl of oatmeal left me wanting.

Today's the day; the day that I will make it to the top of that elevated pyramidal spire, that peak that I have stared at so many times, wishing I could be there. There was always a reason why I couldn't before, not enough time, something more "important" to do in the "real world," or simple lack of motivation. But this time, I have all day to spend with this mountain, no excuses. I pack up my gear and head off. My plan is to make my way around the lake to the base of the crag beneath the vertical cliff overhanging the lake. From there it appears I can follow the talus rock through a chute that will hopefully lead me to the summit.

So far so good. I've made great time with surprisingly little effort.

I am half way up the scree when I notice a yellow-bellied marmot standing in a grassy patch surrounded with Volkswagen size slabs of rock. I dig the camera out of my pack and make my way toward the green island amongst the gray rock. I expect him to retreat as I approached, but he instead comes charging like an African Cape Buffalo. Fortunately, it was just a bluff. As I make my retreat he sits perched high on a rock, watching, making sure I understand that he is the king of this mountain.

Back on track of my original goal, I carefully make my way up through the maze of boulders randomly scattered across the slope. As I approach the summit, my mind races with a mix of emotions. I am expecting a magnificent view, and relieved the uphill is about to finally run out. I make a point to not look outside my immediate area because I dare not spoil the view from the top that I have worked so hard for.

When I get to the top and do look around, I am speechless. There is seemingly endless trees, peaks and beauty. At this moment I have no expectations, worries, or really even thoughts. It is peace, peace in its purest form. Moments like these are so precious to me.

Wilderness is a necessity.

Courtney Bowe was a sophomore in high school when she submitted this for "Voices." She enjoys running cross country, reading, and spending time outdoors with her family and her dog Tikka.

Courtney
Bowe

moments

There are moments when all is still, and all that's felt is pure peace and serenity. Moments when just the surroundings can take a breath away, moments that are meant to be cherished. Nothing can bring that feeling like standing at the top of a mountain, with nature all around you.

It all starts with waking up early, determination set in my mind. At the beginning of the trail, I am a different person. There's one goal for the day and that is to make it to the top. I set out knowing my adventure has just begun. My body is pumped and ready to take on the trail, with my dad right in front of me. As we press on, I look about myself appreciating the beautiful sights and sounds. The birds chirping, trees towering tall, flowers scattered here and there. Sometimes we come upon huckleberries along the trail and we eat them. That is one of the glorious things about living in Montana. You can always have a little treat as you walk. I walk along the trail, stepping over sticks and rocks. Plants brush my legs and tickle my face, I occasionally run into a spider web.

My dad and I are at the halfway mark when we take a break. We take a snack from our packs, drink some water, rest for a few more moments, then we keep moving. I can feel the strain of my muscles as I push them to their limit. I have scratches and I've been bitten by mosquitoes. I am tired, but I know the results will be worth the hard work. My excitement builds as we draw nearer to the end, almost there.

I push my hardest until finally, I've made it. I see beautiful mountains lining up in front of me, all different in their own unique ways. I fill my lungs with the cool, sweet mountain air. I lay down, my head on my pack, knowing I've accomplished my goal. As I lay there, I shut my eyes and feel my surroundings. Everything is so peaceful. I feel the breeze on my skin and the sun shining in my face. I smell the sweet smell of trees and flowers. These are the moments I cherish. The moments that take my stress away, that make me feel like nothing matters except being there on that mountain.

Sandy Compton photo

Leigh Lake from Snowshoe Peak in the Cabinet Mountains Wilderness

Justin Randall was raised in Troy, Montana, and graduated from Troy High School in 2012 as Valedictorian. After seeing a fair section of the rest of the country, he is proud to call Troy his home! He enjoys everything outdoors, a trait forged hiking, fishing and hunting in the Cabinet Mountain Wilderness with his grandfather, Al.

Justin
Randall

wilderness —
source of freedom

To an eleven-year-old boy, growing up in a small town in the mountains of northwest Montana is something akin to long-term summer camp. The amount of freedom a ten-speed, decent sneakers, and a slight inclination for mischief gives you is unsettling. When raised in such a place and fashion, one becomes intimate with the concept of "freedom" at a young age.

Nestled away in the Kootenai National Forest, my friends and I spent our dog days exploring *everything*. A typical afternoon might see us canyoneering Callahan Creek, where we would be swept through narrow shoots, bumping along the bottom with the stones we dislodged. The next day would see us in the forests surrounding our town, turning pilfered nails and discarded boards into forts of such ramshackle grandeur as to make a boy scout blush. When we got the nerve, the old bridge into the Kootenai doubled as a fine place to learn about gravity.

These were the days before our provincial community was burdened with the convenience of cell phones. When we were shooed out of the house each morning it was up to us to make it back in the evening. No one could come calling and even we hardly knew where the next hour would find us.

More than just the advent of the mobile phone, many things have changed since then. The forests are no longer endless, somewhere along the way my friends and I became too logical to trade bruises for the experience of Callahan Creek, and the fence and no trespassing sign erected in front of the old bridge has turned our childhood pastime into a punishable crime.

Many things changed as the world and I grew up, but I never forgot that feeling of unadulterated freedom I learned as a child. To be left to your own wiles to explore the world around you is one of the most pure, fundamental, and increasingly foreign feelings man can experience. It soothes my soul to know that in an atmosphere of continuously accelerating change, there is one place I can still go to get this feeling so fundamental to the human experience. This place is unique in our modern world in that it (and almost it alone) is preserved, meaning that not only I have permanent access to the human experience, but that someday my children and theirs may as well.

This place is, of course, American Wilderness.

Though I have grown to appreciate the convenience afforded by a modern day, first world existence, I have come to terms with the largely tamed, leashed and increasingly docile nature of it. However, I rest easy knowing that I can temporarily escape it all to get my fix of freedom I first savored in the dog days of my youth.

In this summer of 2014, we celebrate fifty years of existence for American Wilderness, and I hope you enjoy the next fifty as much as I plan to.

Happy trails, happy hunting, happy fishing, and happy floating!

Here's to the last best place's last best places.

Sandy Compton photo

Sawtooth Mountain in the proposed Scotchman Peaks Wilderness

voices in the
wilderness

Mark Sheets is a retired Sanders County teacher and the current mayor of Thompson Falls. His story appeared in the *Sanders County Ledger* in January of 2016.

kids, kits, and killer, the wonder dog

Hiking and camping in wild places have been a big part of our family lore. There are many events that are referred to when we are together or on other outings. One memorable one is a wildlife encounter that happened to my youngest son. We took him with us on a backpack trip to Arrowhead Lake in the Cube-Iron Silcox roadless area when he was about a year and a half old. It seemed like a good thing to do for a Fourth of July weekend. My wife carried him with all of the supplies he would need and I carried everything else. I felt like a pack mule but at least my load stayed in one place.

We arrived at the lake and no one was there. Camp was set up very quickly and our son was turned loose to explore the area. Killer, the Wonder Dog, wandered around with him a bit then hit the tent for a nap. I went fishing and my wife just relaxed to enjoy the peace and quiet. It was just what one would have hoped for in getting away from the crowds on the Fourth. After a nice night, the next day would prove to be a bit eventful and make the trip memorable.

The morning was great and the fishing pretty good. At camp in the afternoon, I noticed that the boy was a little odiferous and in need of a diaper change. I called to him, but, as usual, he didn't want to cooperate. He took off at a run directly away from me. He ran around a subalpine tree behind the tent with me after him, and then he gave out a yell. When I rounded the tree, he was nose to nose with a mountain lion — only about a foot away.

It looked like they scared each other about equally. He turned and ran back to me and the lion went in the other direction. My wife heard the commotion and came over and grabbed him while I tried to see where the cat went. It had only gone 20 yards, but did not seem aggressive. My wife came over and we threw rocks at the cat, but it still only went a short way and was soon joined by another one. They seemed to be yearlings, and probably siblings; mom had pushed them out on their own. After some more rock throwing, they finally moved off.

There did not seem to be any mental trauma suffered by the lions or the boy. Through the whole episode Killer stayed in the tent and did not make one little peep. For a yappy Chihuahua, it was an amazing show of self-preservation.

The rest of the day was uneventful but that changed in the night. It started to rain and that changed to snow. We woke up to a couple of inches on the ground. This was not mentioned on the weather report before we left home. We figured that it would quit soon and then dry out. It rained all day.

Spending a rainy day in a two person tent with a child and another adult was a bit challenging, needless to say. Naptime was good and there was time to relax and read, but it was too short. It rained all night. The next day, we knew something would have to be done, because diapers were almost all used up. My wife wrapped the boy in what we had that would keep him dry and headed out and I stuffed everything else in the pack and followed. It was a wet and miserable trip out for us but we survived just fine.

As we look back and reflect on that trip, the encoun-
ter with the mountain lions was really amazing. We were probably the first humans that they had encountered and it seemed like they were just curious. As to backpacking with a child, the next time, we would wait until he was a bit older, out of diapers and able to walk on his own. Weather seems to always add to the adventure and no matter how prepared you are, it always throws you a curve ball. Lastly, Killer is worthless as a guard dog. She would throw you under the bus to save herself.

Jared Winslow was the 2014
winner of the Friends of Scotchman Peaks
Wilderness essay scholarship competition
for Libby High School.

family tradition

July in northwest Montana is a time for exploration.
Cool mornings and hot afternoons mirror the stark contrast in topography
one can find by simply hiking for a few hours into the Cabinet Mountain
Wilderness Area. The slow meanders of the Bull River are quickly replaced
with the waterfalls and pools of Rock Creek. My father and I decided it was
time for a change from the warm waters and large-mouth bass of Bull Lake,
to snow fed Rock Creek, as well as Rock Lake, and some westslope cutthroat.

Family conversation around the evening camp fire at "the Lake" is a way to
let the body and mind unwind from the days' activities, as well as an opportunity for the older family members to tell stories about various adventures they
have had. It was in this format that the Rock Lake hike for my dad and me
came about. Cabinet Mountain Wilderness maps were brought out from the
glove box of the pickup and through the yellow light of the Coleman lantern,
the decision was made to hike to Rock Lake and up to St. Paul Pass. Here we
would spend the night, and if we were up for it the next morning, we would

try for Libby Lakes. Our exit route from the wilderness would be the St. Paul Peak trail, where my grandfather would be waiting for us.

The excitement built the entire day as all the details of the trip were planned. Food, tents, sleeping bags, fishing gear, bear spray, mosquito repellant, and cooking gear found their way into the packs. As we got ready to go, my dad used phrases and words like "minimalist" when referring to our pack load, and "leave no trace" that we had visited the wilderness. He told me that hiking and fishing and using the "wilderness" invoked a level of land use responsibility and practices that needed to be followed, so other people and generations could have experiences like the one we were about to have.

My grandpa drove us to the trail head. We started hiking up the trail, looking at all the trees and how the sunlight seemed to dance off the limbs. As we were hiking, we heard Rock Creek running below us and went down to fish.

In the crystal clear water we could see fish and caught ten in a short amount of time. It was great. Once we were finished there, we kept hiking to the lake. We ate huckleberries as we enjoyed the beauty of the hike and the fresh air of the mountains. As soon as we got to Rock Lake, we fished and caught a few in the blue water. St. Paul Pass was around the backside of the lake, so we began to work our way around. There was no trail; we had to try to pick the best route.

Sometimes we were in boulder fields above the tree line, and at times we were right at the edge of the lake. At one point, we went close to the water because that was the best route. We ended up falling in, but it was all part of the fun. Once we got around the lake, we went up toward the pass to our camping spot. We set up camp and ate in the pass and talked about the day.

At twilight, we saw mule deer and elk and heard a bull elk bugle. It was a crystal clear night and the sheer rock face of Ojibway Peak glowed in the moonlight. It was awesome! Then next morning, we woke up and went down the back side of Saint Paul Pass. We rock hopped down the pass to Saint Paul Lake, where we fished again. After fishing and examining the back side of Saint Paul Peak, which is breathtaking, we went down the trail and eventually back home.

Hiking into Rock Lake with my dad was an experience that I will never forget. The fishing, huckleberries, mountains, bugling elk, and fresh air all made the experience one I want to repeat. The wilderness is a place where I want to someday take my children. This year, in celebration of the 50th anniversary of the Wilderness Act, we are planning a hike to Wanless Lake. It is here that we will continue the father and son tradition we started and immensely enjoyed - an overnight hike in the wilderness.

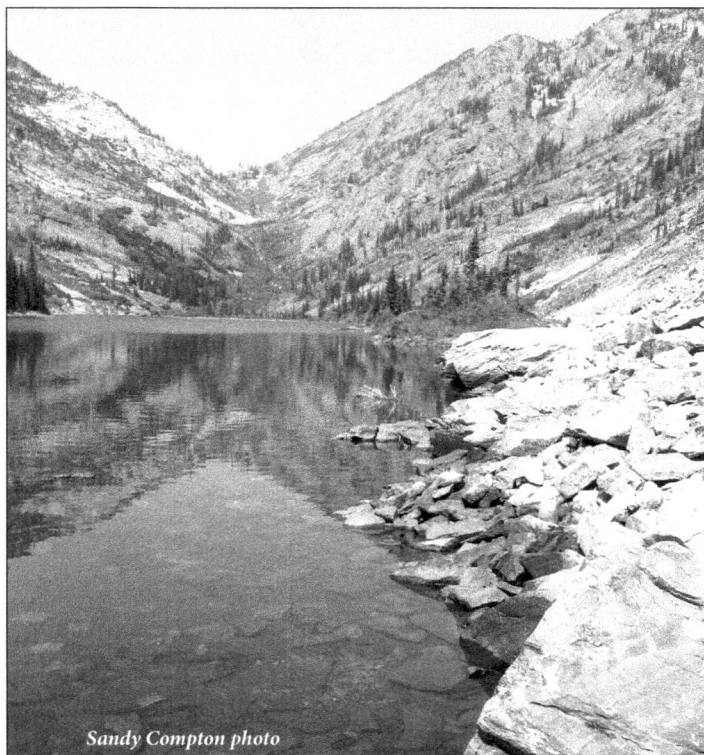

Sandy Compton photo

Rock Lake with St. Paul Pass reflected.

voices in the
wilderness

Megan Hight graduated from Troy High School in 2014. This essay won the annual Friends of Scotchman Peaks Wilderness scholarship competition at Troy High School.

real beauty

The time had come. I was the oldest child; my dad had been waiting my whole life for this moment and I wasn't about to let him down now by not going with. It was the first day of hunting season, and the air was chilly. We had gone to the shooting range, practicing, and all that practice leading up to this day. It was my time to shine. We pack the essentials, grab the guns and we were out the door; the frigid morning air nipping at my nose. It's not yet light outside, and we drive for what seems like forever. I will never forget the setting; my dad driving down the road, the heat blasting because I wanted to get internally warm, he kept playing "Watching Airplanes" by Gary Allen over and over because it was the one I knew best. That moment will be engraved in my mind forever.

We arrived at our "secret hunting spot," as my dad called it, and we hopped out, making sure to shut the doors quietly. The cold air hit me like a freight train. I instantly regretted my decision to try and get "internally warm." As I stood there, looking at the massive mountain we were about to climb, all I could feel was excitement. Being with two of the things I loved most; my dad and nature. We were off on our grand adventure.

Growing up, I always went on hikes with my family, but having two younger siblings we always took it slow. My dad did not hold back when he signed us up for this hike. Straight up the mountain we went. Before every hike, we would always pack a little food fuel. As we were hiking, I tried my best to keep quiet while I reached around to my pack to grab the mini snickers bar I had packed for my lunch. Obviously, I wasn't doing such a good job at keeping quiet, when my dad turned around. At first, I felt a little sheepish, grabbing into my pack when it wasn't even lunch time, but then I saw the look on my dad's face. He looked at me, smiled, reached in his pack and grabbed his baby snickers out as well. We stopped and ate our baby snickers in the peace and quiet before we trekked back on up the mountain.

Before reaching the top of that mountain, I had thought I had seen beauty in the world. You go around; you see a horse running freely through a pasture, that's beauty. You're driving down the road, and you see a deer and her fawn, that's beauty. But when I reached the top of that mountain, I didn't even have a word in mind. Speechless. I had never seen anything so beautiful in all my young life and I still don't think I ever will. Looking down on everything, all misty, with the sun peeking through the clouds hitting the earth just right, it was all I could do to just stand there in awe. I looked over to my dad, thinking he'd be looking at the same view as me, but when I looked his direction, I met his eyes, and I knew this was going to be a day I would never forget. And right then I understood why my dad had waited for this moment my whole life.

Sandy Compton photo

Hiking an elk trail on the Emily Crag
in the proposed Scotchman Peaks Wilderness

voices in the
wilderness

Tony Brown is a life-long resident of Troy, Montana, and the former mayor of said city. This is only one of his many good stories. It was published in *The Western News*.

Tony
Brown

bad medicine
is good medicine

The Lincoln/Sanders County Line has a little-known, unique distinction. It divides Bull Lake from Bull River. These are separated by a quarter mile and 20 feet of elevation. Bull River drains the west side of the Cabinet Mountains Wilderness and runs south. Bull Lake is fed by Ross Creek and the Scotchman Peaks. Lake Creek drains Bull Lake and runs north to the Kootenai River.

Growing up in Troy, we thought of hunting and fishing as the Yaak River or the Lake Creek. Lake Creek was the place to catch big bull trout and prime whitetail hunting. My best buddy lived on Highway 56, so I became familiar with Lake Creek. I camped on Bull Lake before there were designated campgrounds, hosts or FEES. Campers sat at the fire and Hank Williams songs were resurrected from the night. My children swam in Bull Lake as babies. I don't doubt that our youngest was conceived on its shores.

I've also camped at the lake when mosquitoes were so bad they would carry you away. On two occasions, micro-bursts destroyed our campsite.

When I put myself into a pair of moccasins 500 years in the past, I know pitching my tipi in a swamp wouldn't be best. But, behind Bad Medicine Campground, just up Emma Gulch in the Spires, it's warm and dry with outcroppings to protect from weather and fresh water. And, it's hidden.

When white men encountered the Indians, they asked, "How's the hunting?" The Indians answered, "No good, bad medicine, don't go there." To this day it's known as Bad Medicine. The story of a rockslide burying an Indian camp was made up to keep white men from poking around.

There is no vantage point that allows a full perspective of the Bad Medicine Spires, unless you hike in, which I have several times. Approaching from the north on Highway 56, only a third of the Spires are visible. When traveling north on 56, the south face is visible. From across Bull Lake, the Spires appear to be a continuous cliff face. They are actually walls that run perpendicular to Bull Lake. The mountain between the Spires and Bull Lake is larger than mountains on either side of the Kootenai River at Troy. The valley between that mountain and the Spires is larger than the valley in which Troy is located, yet the valley isn't visible from any road.

Thirty years ago, my wife Val and I were on a moonlight canoe ride when I looked up and saw the moon shining through a spire. Around the spire, green lights blinked as though from an alien craft. From Dorr Skeels, we watched the lights ascend out of sight behind Mount Vernon.

For a time, I thought I'd seen two spires positioned so as to give the illusion of a hole — a hole through sheer rock was too incredible. Besides, I thought someone would have discovered it already, and I'd never heard of holes through the cliffs at Bad Medicine. For that matter, I'd never heard of anyone who'd hiked into the Spires. I knew then I'd have to hike into the Spires and see for myself.

My first attempt was up the mine adit road from the Ross Creek Cedars road and off the end of a switchback halfway up the mountain. After hours of hiking, I became increasingly frustrated. I tried to follow the ridgeline, only to find wall after wall hundreds of feet high. To keep going, I would have to backtrack around the top. I was getting no closer to the hole I'd seen.

For my next attempt, I studied a Forest Service map —this was before Google Earth, — and there were no trails. From Bad Medicine intersection on Ross Creek Cedars Road, I headed into the brush. I reached a shale slide and began along the base of the cliffs, two steps up and one back. And, I found my first hole in a spire. I wasn't even close to the one I'd seen from the lake.

On my next adventure into the Spires, I went in from the north end. I canoed across the lake from Angel Island and bushwhacked up Emma Gulch. I remember pushing into the hidden valley and seeing for the first time the full enormity and height of the spires and cliffs.

A small stream tumbles down 30 feet where the ridgeline meets the draw. I thought I was in Shangri-La. A mountain goat grazed high up on Bull Mountain, the mountain between Bull Lake and Hidden Valley. There — they have names. The sun rose higher over Snowshoe and shadows crept down the cliffs and spires. At every minute new images appeared, dancing down the walls. I saw a Chief's profile with deep-set eyes and large prominent nose shadowed above a warm morning smile. Comfortable and serene, I knew I was not the first to stand on that ground.

I could also see clearly how Bad Medicine was formed — not a catastrophic event that occurred in a heartbeat. Bull Mountain is slowly sliding east. It will eventually push across the narrows south of Angel Island, and there will be two Bull Lakes, North and South. The waters of South will spill over the divide at the County Line, and South Bull Lake and Bull River will be united. North Bull Lake will become marshland and ponds.

For nine more hours, I hiked up the ridge, climbing around wall after wall. Half way up, I rested under a huge cedar tree growing out of the cliff, as big and old as any in the Ross Creek grove, clinging to the rock and arching skyward for hundreds of years. It was further evidence of Bull Mountain inching away from Mount Vernon.

I timed this hike to coincide with the full moon. If there was a hole in the Spires, and I wanted to photograph the moon through it. I wasn't able to take that picture, but one of my best photos is of a campfire perched at the very top of Bad Medicine, 15 feet from a 400-foot drop. I lay in my sleeping bag in a patch of huckleberries, grazing on berries and watching a full moon light the snowcapped peaks of the Cabinets. I slept well.

In morning light, from the edge of the cliff, I found myself looking directly through the hole in the spire I was searching for, like the eye of a giant needle. I edged my way out to get a photo and saw there were holes in other spires. I began to see that each wall had a hole or a notch, lined up as if a missile had made them, all the way from the first hole I found the year before to the top of the highest spire.

If that doesn't make the hair stand up on the back of your neck, nothing will.

Did a comet crash through the Spires? Did softer rock captured like the core of a Twinkie melt away, leaving holes skipping from wall to wall in a perfectly straight line? Did a juvenile delinquent alien in his father's Quantum Millennium Terraplane doing a fly-by shooting ten million years ago?

Bad Medicine Spires is a magical and mysterious place. If you visit, go with humility and respect. Watch every step you take. A fall will be unforgiving. Sit quietly, open your eyes and you will see many things.

Tony Brown Photo

The hole in the spires.

voices in the
wilderness

Emma McConnaughey was the 2014 *overall winner of the Friends of Scotchman Peaks Wilderness High School Scholarship contest. She likes to play in Callahan Creek.*

a life saving event

We were almost there. After hours of driving along steep mountain roads and deep ravines our destination was in sight: Callahan Creek. My friend Lizzie and I had been waiting all summer for this trip. For the first time we were going camping together. We had everything planned; we would sleep in our own tent away from my family; we would fish, explore, stalk "prey," and maybe go for a swim.

Setting up camp was simple. My parents and I had been there to scope out the site just a couple weeks before, so we already had everything planned. Tents went up, fires were made, and dinner was cooking. Hotdogs and marshmallows roasted beside each other on separate branches of the same stick. A night well spent.

Our one whole day there began with a hot cup of coffee. Let's face it. You can't start the day without coffee, even while camping. After coffee was fishing. Lizzie and I assembled our poles, picked our hand-made flies, and cast off. No luck. We moved farther downstream, but there were too many rapids for any decent sized fish, so we tried upstream, but now the water was too calm and did not have enough cover.

We returned to our original place, but as we cast once again, a flurry of feathers caught our attention. A young swallow was just learning to fly and had fallen right into the middle of the river. Of course we tossed aside our poles and rushed to its aid. After seizing our newfound friend from the uncaring clutches of the near-freezing water, Lizzie and I ran back to our camp as fast as our gangly teenage legs would carry us. We caught bugs and gathered seeds and breadcrumbs (a motley collection seeing as how at the time we had no idea what a swallow would eat) and filled a medicine cup with water. We sat with the bird and kept it company until its feathers were dry.

Once the bird was acting perky again, we carried it to a spot on the rocky shore near where we had first found it and placed it on a boulder. Shrieks of terror! Lizzie and I both fell back as the bird jumped and flew up between us to a tree branch above our heads and started chirping and squealing for its mother. We assumed that if the bird was rude enough to scare us it obviously must be feeling well enough to be left alone.

I retrieved my fishing pole from where it had fallen and cast off again. No luck whatsoever. Lizzie cast. No fish. I could see them, just a few feet away, and cast again. My fly landed just above two fish between two rocks. Yes! This time for sure. There was no way they could pass this up. And yet they did. Blood rushed to my face and my eyes blazed. That was it. No more nice fishing. I threw aside my pole, (nearly hitting Lizzie in the face in the process,) and dove. Score! I stood, dripping, scratched, and bruised, with a fish in my hands. I proudly carried my prize to the other side of the creek. Just as I was stepping out of the water—oh, horror!—I lost my footing and slipped. The fish went flying. I jumped up the moment I slammed into the ground. There he was, flopping frantically in a shallow pool. I snatched him up again and, pride forgotten, carried him to our camp.

After depositing the fish into my mother's care, I returned to the water, gathered my fishing gear, and promptly caught a second fish with my hands. This one I lost, but he was too small anyways. Lizzie and I carried our supplies to our tent and settled down for a dinner of fresh caught fish and more hotdogs under a glorious sunset.

Sometimes I still wonder, "Whatever happened to that swallow?" Did he make it? Did his mother accept him after being handled by humans? I don't know. I never will. All I know is that I didn't let him drown, and I can be proud of that.

Don Clark retired from Libby
School District after many years as a teacher.
He has also taught many people about hunting
in Wilderness, and loves to hunt and recreate
in and around the Cabinet Moutains Wilderness.

hunting wilderness

I came to Libby, Montana from South Dakota in 1967. I was unfamiliar with the concept of Wilderness. My wife drew a mountain goat permit in 1969 and we began hiking into the wilderness in search of "The Beast the color of Winter."

Since then, I have spent a lifetime appreciating the waterfalls, lakes, rocky cirques, sheer cliffs, wildflowers, animals and solitude of Wilderness. Friends and I have hiked much of the Cabinet Mountain Wilderness that was established in 1964. As avid hunters, we have harvested elk, bears, deer, mountain lions, bobcat, moose, bighorn rams and mountain goats in the quietness of the wilderness. When you draw a moose, goat or sheep permit for the wilderness you have to hunt there.

It sounds like the hunting is spectacular in the wilderness. Actually, the elk hunting can be very difficult because of the steep terrain and the distances you have to hike to get to the game. This holds doubly-true for packing out animals over long distances. But, because it is more physical than many want to endure, the area is not crowded. Usually you have it pretty much to yourself. It sets one apart from the regular hunters who spend a lot of time driving.

What *is* spectacular are the cliffs, lakes, glaciers, and wildness of the area. We have also been fortunate to see wolves, wolverine, coyotes, pica, martin, fisher, porcupine, eagles, loon, grizzlies, geese and grouse while hiking the wilderness.

As a forest service trail crew summer worker I helped fight fire in the wilderness and helped clear the trails with a double bit ax and cross-cut saw so others could more easily reach the high lakes and see the panoramic vistas. My time spent as a hunter, recreational hiker, and trail crew worker built an appreciation of wilderness in my soul, and I think anyone could share my love of land set aside as God created it if they experienced it like I have.

Courtesy Don Clark

A wilderness bull elk.

voices in the
wilderness

Carla Parks is a hiker, fisher and former mayor of Thompson Falls. Her essay appeared in the *Sanders County Ledger*.

"easy" isn't a way to a mountain lake.

Dan and I moved to this paradise in the winter of 1976. I grew up on the Clearwater River in Idaho. My Dad was a packer and a guide above the Selway River, so I have always loved the woods. But I experienced mountain travel from the back of a horse.

At the time of our move we had a newborn son who kept me tied to the house until his feet were negotiating firm ground. Then the call of the forest could once more be answered. I found a notice in the paper about a guided hike up to St Paul's Lake from the Bull River side. They classified it as an "easy" hike. Great. The children should be fine. I never worried a minute about Dan's or my abilities.

We started the hike among jovial people with a knowledgeable guide. She seemed kind at first. The valley forest was lush green, and welcomed us with smells of verdant moisture and the sweet scent of fir. We wandered along a shaded trail, and I was loving it. Then we came to the creek. There was a large log that the other hikers scampered across. My confidence quickly plummeted. I was afraid of heights. I looked at the cold creek and wading didn't seem to be a good idea. So Dan coaxed me up on the lofty tree and I crept across.

Okay, that was over. I didn't look forward to the return trip, but the lake was just a short jaunt ahead —I thought — and I eagerly anticipated that. We left the shaded green of the bottom and headed up a hill. Not too bad. Then it got steeper, and the sun got higher. I looked up the mountain, and there above me was a trail that possessed a myriad of switchbacks. The log made me doubt the classification of an "easy" hike, but the mountain and the switchbacks solidified my feelings.

The kids and Dan trooped on in front, though, and I was tough. Resolute, I went forward. We kept getting higher on what I remember was an endless hot trudge. Finally, sweating profusely, I sat down. I told Dan and the boys to continue. I would follow after I was rested —with absolutely no self-assurance that was going to happen in any reasonable length of time. There I sat, but in ten minutes, my gumption came back, and I slogged my way to the top. When I came over the rise, the lake reflected that dark blue sky that only can be found in the high mountains. The rock bowl that held the lake was stunning. It was magic. The clear, cold water washed my sweat away. Suddenly the hike seemed easier. I was hooked.

Since that day, I have made a hundred trips or more to the lakes that are scattered like gems throughout this area. I have had hikes filled with white tree spires reaching like church steeples to perfect skies; huckleberries giving that tart sweetness that always calls for more; bears and the adrenaline and wonder that always follow upon seeing them; carpets of purple, white, and yellow flowers beneath my feet; and forests filled with the dusty smell and wondrous sight of beargrass in mass blooms. I have herded children up mountains and seen them collapse under a big tree totally exhausted — lamenting that their parents would do such torture. Then they find a likely limb and start a charge up the trail to fight off the dragons that menace us. We come to those amazing lakes from which, on the right days, we catch the red-sided trout and see the glue-footed goats on the cliff surrounding. We settle in to dig through our packs for the tastiest morsels that ever existed and lounge on big rocks or soft moss for an afternoon respite. Then we reluctantly go down the mountain and home. Not one of these treks were "easy."

So, be warned, those of you who are new to this area and hear or read of an "easy" hike to a mountain lake. Don't believe it for a moment. Anything that wonderful has to be earned.

voices in the
wilderness

Jim Mellen photo

Pete Mickelson lives in Alaska in the summer and winters in the balmy confines of Lincoln County. Cedar Lakes (left) were his first fishing trip in the Cabinet Mountains Wilderness.

Pete
Mickelson

why I like wilderness

I grew up in two places: first on a farm on the edge of the Allegheny National Forest in northwest Penn's Woods and then on the edge of the Cabinets in Libby.

As a boy, from age 6 to 12, I fished for brook trout on a stream with no houses or visible skid trails for its length until it reached the Allegheny River. Although there probably were old logging trails and selective logging along the stream, to me it was wilderness.

I moved to Montana to attend Forestry school, but finished with a degree in Wildlife Biology. Uncle Carl Schmiedel introduced me to fishing in Lincoln County at Burke Lake, close the BC border and no trail for the near-mile hike from the end of Pete Creek road. The lake was a pearl set in a fairly open forest with rocky slopes extending above the tree line. The 24" brook trout there (stocked by a friend of Carl's) were more than twice as long as the largest brookie I ever caught back East. To me, this was true wilderness — beyond the end of the road, a beautiful untouched lake with no trail to it, and no signs of humans.

Finally, my uncle took me to the Cabinets — first to Cedar Lakes, and then to my favorite, Wanless, accessed via Libby Creek. Trails led to the crest of the Cabinets, but we bushwhacked to reach Wanless and its fine cutthroat fishing.

I liked being alone, except for the companionship of and wisdom imparted by my uncle. During grouse season, my favorite hunting area was Flatiron, accessed from Pipe Creek road or from a grown-over cat trail, but no regular foot or ski trails like there are now. Now trails allow travel, meaning more people and more competition for game (and fish).

Foresters Russ Hudson and Mel Parker instructed me regarding timber cruising, and I got to see a diversity of timbered country owned by St. Regis Paper Company. Often we had to hike a few miles beyond the end of the road to reach our plots in fairly wild country.

Now I split my time between the northern limit of the Pacific coastal rainforest and the Libby area. Home in Alaska is on a beach ridge with 100-foot-tall western hemlocks and Sitka spruce and a view of the Copper River estuary, barrier islands, open Pacific, and the 3,000-foot mountains of Hinchinbrook Island in Prince William Sound. My house is built around and anchored by a 3-foot diameter spruce with a crow's nest 65 feet up. It provides an even better view of surrounding wild country. It's not unsullied. I can see a cell phone tower and wind generator six miles away on a 1000-foot hill on Hinchinbrook, a former White Alice communications site similar to most Dew Line sites built in the mid-1950s around the perimeter of Alaska.

My best wilderness experience in Alaska is hiking on a barrier island along the Pacific on a rainless day in May or June, cruising the waters of Prince William Sound, or, better yet, a bird's eye view at 700 feet from a Super Cub of the wild coast or nearby Wrangell-St. Elias National Park and Preserve. I hunt deer on Hawkins Island four miles away from home with a view of the Mummy Islands and Egg Islands in outer Orca Inlet. I don't cross over the top of the island because once I saw an oil tanker headed for the oil port of Valdez (Cordovans call it Vile Disease). I treasure the unsullied view of the wild country to the east with the occasional glimpse of Kayak Island. It's 60 miles to the southeast, where Stellar became the first Caucasian (with Bering in 1741) to set foot in Alaska and for whom a jay and a sea lion amongst other fauna and flora are named.

If I get to Libby early in October, I hike into the Cabinets, perhaps to Leigh Lake or up Scenery Mountain trail. Now that I'm in my 60s, hiking a trail instead of balancing on downed trees and stepping over windfall makes it a bit easier. I spend more time looking for Clark's nutcrackers and blue grouse, or perhaps looking for elk tracks, beds and other signs of this species that favor mostly roadless, mountainous country here in Lincoln County — at least in late summer and early fall.

I envy bowhunters who go after elk, goats and bighorns in the Cabinets or at help spot and then pack out meat as does Don Clark every fall. I have to be content with hunting grouse or a quick trip over to Freezeout Lake to hunt pheasants with a backdrop of the Bob Marshall country in the Rockies.

I still prefer to hunt, fish and photograph alone, to enjoy the scenery and wildlife and to know that I'm either in wilderness or at least close to it. Although I still harvest timber, mostly for firewood, I'm strongly in favor of setting aside wilderness, certainly in the high country like the Cabinets, parts of the Yaak, and Scotchman Peaks.

When he is not in the woods or on the stage, Keith Meyers owns and operates the Magic Wrench in Libby, Montana.

Keith
Meyers

all new to me

This was all new to me.

I had been invited to go with several friends and a new member of our community on a day hike to a little lake up in the Cabinet Mountains Wilderness. Nothing really "new" about that, I had been hiking plenty in the woods.

But, always in the past, my hikes had been means to an end, trying to get somewhere. It was work getting there, setting up camp, getting wood and shelter. Hurry, hurry. Almost always "somewhere" was a lake or stream with fish. This hike was different. This lake didn't have any fish. I wasn't sure why we were going there. Boy, did I have a lot to learn.

When we got out of the rig, the October morning was crisp and clear, but felt downright cold after the long summer. Almost immediately we crossed a small stream that required some fancy footwork. While three of our party made it across with slightly damp shoes, the forth member apparently found the water inviting, and took a brief swim. We won't say who.

Soon the trail faded away along with the everyday worries of the world, and after a few hours we found ourselves sprawled on a hillside of bear grass, gear spread around us, a small lake below. The sun warmed our bodies, coffee and conversation warmed our souls, and the more elder members of our little tribe settled down for what looked like a long winter's nap. I must say, it was an inviting thought, but the lake and a snowfield tucked up against the mountain begged exploring. Down I went.

The closer I got to the lake, the more the snowfield called to me. What was I seeing? A cave in the snow, perhaps big enough for a school bus, had been created as the water came down the mountainside. Up I went.

Inside, I stayed very quiet, not sure if a loud noise would bring problems I didn't want to think about. How many years had this snow been here, hiding in the shadows of the mountain? Sitting in the cave, looking down its length at the lake below and the sunshine on the hillside across the lake was magical. But cold. The sunshine, coffee and friends looked pretty good. Winter was coming and I would get plenty of cold then.

The hike out was uneventful — except for one member, the same member — of our group who found a log across a creek too slippery. Again, nothing was hurt but pride. Again, we won't say who.

If you have never napped in the sunshine in the bear grass on a cool fall day, you don't know what you're missing. I sure didn't, up till then. Maybe it's because my legs have got a few miles on them now, or maybe it's because my soul needs the nourishment, but now my trips into the mountains almost always include some time doing nothing. Often in bear grass. Often — actually always — with coffee. Or under an old cedar tree, with it's branches sheltering me from the rain that is too often following me around. On a ridge top, watching, sometimes for hours, the nothingness and the everything that surrounds me. The nothingness cleanses my soul, the everything fills me with its beauty and grace, and I hike back down.

We are so blessed.

*Glacier lilies under the permanent snowfield in Melissa Basin in
the proposed Scotchman Peaks Wilderness.*

voices in the
wilderness

Ashley South grew up in beautiful Troy, Montana. She graduated from Troy High School in 2012 and attended Flathead Valley Community College for one year. She is married to Anthony South, "man of her dreams." They live in the Yaak Valley with their dog Violet. Ashley works for Montana Wilderness Association as the Lincoln County Outreach Coordinator.

i wanted an adventure and I got one

Lying under the oldest cedar tree in our back yard,
I begin to reminisce about our trip from the previous weekend; wind-swept peaks, craggy cliffs, and the high alpine midnight-blue lake. It seems dream-like until I shift my achy knees and sunburned skin. I ponder why the truest sense of contentment I have come to know is only achievable while in these wild places. I guess the answer to pure contentment will have to wait, but for now the love for wilderness and our mind-blowing adventures are reason enough to endure achy knees and sunburned skin.

The weekend before: Beep, beep, beep! The sound of our alarm wakes my stiff muscles and sleepy eyes. I roll out of bed and excitement slowly permeated my body. I can't pack or eat breakfast fast enough.

voices in the
wilderness

As we crawl into our beat up '92 Honda civic I begin to question if I have brought enough food and water, if I'm physically fit enough for this adventure, and will the good weather stick around long enough to reach the summit.

My mind clears as we reach the trail head. We throw on our packs and head up the trail. The first mile is full of anticipation and waking muscles. "Pace yourself" my husband says "It's going to be a long day".

Before I know it, I am gazing up at a 8,742-foot peak. I feel a rush of adrenaline throughout my body as Anthony says "Let's do this."

Snowshoe Peak looked intimidating, but I wanted an adventure and I got it. As we scramble over Bockman Peak we realized we had taken the path less traveled. From there, Snowshoe towered over neighboring peaks and welcomed us with her craggy cliffs and glacier cut beauty. From a distance, we spotted two white dots roaming around in a small alpine meadow. Mountain goats! We went to take a closer look. As time passed, we just sat watching and experiencing their beauty and way of life. Sitting in awe, we observed how amazing these animals truly are to be calling this beautiful place home.

Exertion, sweat, pushing physical limits and absolute breathtaking scenery describe the next few hours. We reach the rounded summit and look out from the heart of the Cabinet Mountain Wilderness. Sitting completely immersed in unending beauty, I realize this is why wilderness and wild places are essential for now and for future generations.

We took our time on the descent, eating whortleberries and drinking the fresh snowmelt, savoring our surroundings. As we reached the valley floor, I found myself connected to this place in a way words can never describe. Each step taken deeper into a wild place will allow every person to be immersed and replenished with a deeper sense of realness and enlightenment. I am thankful for Snowshoe Peak and the adventure it led us on.

Ashley South with Snowshoe Peak and Blackwell Glacier in the Cabinet Mountains Wilderness.

voices in the
wilderness

Austin Johnson wrote the best essay from Noxon High School for the 2015 Friends of Scotchman Peaks Wilderness scholarship essay competition. The picture at left is of the hike out from Little Spar. His story appeared in the *Sanders County Ledger* in July of 2016.

Austin
Johnson

fish(es) on!

My most memorable wilderness experience was when my father, my younger brother Aaron, my friend Zane Onofrey, and I hiked to Little Spar lake for a weekend of camping, fishing, and the great outdoors. We left early in the morning so that we wouldn't have to hike during the heat of the day. We drove from our house in Noxon and then up to the trail where we got out and began our hike. The hike to Little Spar is a four-mile hike and is not a very difficult hike, in fact it's quite a fun hike with lots of beautiful scenery.

We started to hike through the forest at the bottom of the trail looking at all the big trees and wondering how long they had been there. After a while the trees began to get thinner and we found ourselves following the creek that flows from Little Spar down to Big Spar. There were parts of the stream that were still covered by ice, and we were hiking to the lake in July.

We would look across the valley hoping that we would see some mountain goats as we were hiking up to the lake but we didn't. We got to the point where you could see the bowl where the lake was ahead of us and we started talking about how much fun the fishing was going to be. When we got to the lake we pitched our tents on a good flat spot and set up the fire so when we came back with fish they would be ready to cook. Then we were off to the water for fishing.

We each took our poles down to the lake and looked for a good spot. We found two big rocks near the creek and decided on that spot. We climbed up onto the rocks, pulled out our bait and cast out our hooks. On my very first cast I caught a little cutthroat trout, I pulled the hook out and put it back in the water. I knew then that it would be a very fun trip if we were already on the fish. We fished for about two hours and between the four of us we caught over 50 fish. It was an incredible first day of our trip.

We took two fish for each person back to the camp for dinner for the night. The fish were delicious. After dinner we sat around the campfire and talked about our day and how much fun we had, later we went to our tents so that we could get some rest for the next day and the hike down.

We woke up in the morning and after some coffee and berries were off to fishing again. This time we went a different way around the lake and found another large rock that we could stand on and see the fish from. This spot was much different though. The last spot we fished was very shallow and you could see everything, even the fish. This new spot was very deep and all you could see was the aqua blue of the water and the rock that jutted into the water below us.

We all four fished in the same spot this time, spread out across the same rock. I cast straight out into the deep dark water with no idea of knowing what was out there. My first cast I didn't catch one but when I pulled my bait out of the water I saw one chasing it so I dropped my bait back in really quick.

What happened next was unheard of. I felt the fish bite the hook so I set the hook, then when I got it close to the rock I saw two fish on my line, I was confused on how I had two fish with only one hook. I pulled them onto the rock and everyone else looked with the same look of astonishment. One fish had the hook and the other held onto my sinker the entire fight in.

That had never happened to any of us before and we all thought that was a great way to cap off an awesome trip. After another hour or so we packed all of our stuff up and hiked back to the truck. That was my most memorable wilderness experience.

Sandii Mellen photo

Fishing at the outlet of Little Spar Lake.

voices in the
wilderness

Mahala Wedel's essay was submitted to the annual 2015 Friends of Scotchman Peaks Scholarship essay competition, and published in *The Western News* in April of 2015.

bramlet birthday

July 28, 2014, marked my Grandma Wedel's 80th
birthday. The entire extended family tried to decide how to best celebrate
this historic event. Since the summer months in Montana provide wonderful weather, beautiful scenery, and many recreational opportunities,
everyone agreed to travel up to Montana to spend a week of family togeth-
erness, exploring the wilderness, and the surrounding lakes and rivers.
People made the journey from all parts of the country, including Indiana,
Wisconsin, and Kansas to join together at my home in Libby, Montana.
Many of the younger relatives had never been to this area and therefore
never had the opportunity to experience the mountain wilderness.

This week of celebration was spent engaging in softball, volleyball,
floating the Kootenai River, along with tubing and water skiing on
Thompson Lake. A full day of swimming and picnicking at Howard Lake
was also enjoyed. One of the highlights of the week's activities was a day
hike to Bramlet Lake in the Cabinet Wilderness. While sitting around the

backyard bonfire one evening, we discussed preparations for the following day's excursion. As the details of the hike were planned, the anticipation and the excitement grew.

Early in the morning, packs were filled with water, snacks, mosquito repellent, and extra clothing. Family members drove to the Bramlet Lake trailhead, as we started our adventure for the day. It was a clear crisp morning in the mountains of Montana. Shortly after walking up the trail, we noticed an abundance of huckleberries. The "out-of-towners" were amazed by the prevalence and flavor of this mountain snack. Throughout the hike we would often stop and enjoy this unique, tasty berry. Along the way we paused several times to take pictures and gazed at the magnificent scenery. I felt fortunate that I lived in such a beautiful area and was proud to be able to share such a place with my extended family. Many commented on the spectacular and unspoiled beauty of this place I called home.

After approximately two hours on the trail, which was sometimes very steep, we arrived at our destination, Bramlet Lake. The pristine lake was as cold as the mountain air. The reflection of the mountains peaks could be seen in the crystal clear water. We then noticed a waterfall on the opposite side of the lake gently falling across a rock face. Some made their way around the lake to explore; some bravely waded into the water, and the rest tried their luck at fishing. When we came together later in the afternoon to enjoy our snacks, we were all in awe of this breathtaking wilderness and acknowledged that 2014 marked the 50th anniversary of its formation. I felt a sense of appreciation to those, that so many years ago, had the foresight to preserve these special areas. I also realized that we all have a responsibility to continue to protect this beautiful land. In the spirit of preservation, we left nothing behind, packing out all of our containers and wrappers. Before we headed back down the trail, we took a family picture in front of Bramlet Lake. We also paused at several viewpoints for additional photos to forever capture the memories of this special time together. And, of course, we stopped many times on the way down the trail to devour more huckleberries.

It was a grand way to celebrate both my Grandmother's 80th birthday, and the 50th anniversary of the Cabinet Mountains Wilderness.

Rachel Rebo was the 2015
Scotchman Peaks scholarship essay competition winner for Libby High School, as well as the overall winner for all eight participating Montana and Idaho high schools.

climbing dome, finding home

My name is Rachel Rebo and I was born and raised in Libby, Montana. Growing up in this beautiful town, it's hard not to fall in love with the outdoors. Looking back on my childhood, it seems as if there was never a moment where I wanted to be inside, no matter what the weather was like. As I grew older, hiking is what really caught my interest. It helped me to physically grow stronger and at the same time, enjoy the environment I am so blessed to have grown up in. I have hiked a lot of trails and have seen so many amazing views, but none of them have taken my breath away like Dome Mountain did.

I was first introduced to the idea of hiking Dome Mountain in my A.P. Senior Government class in September 2014. That Saturday at 8:00 a.m. my boyfriend and I began what I believe was the best hike of my life.

The main trail, leading to lower Cedar Lake, wasn't anything out of the ordinary until we made our way into the shadiest part of the trail. Further ahead, huckleberries were everywhere, which is why I believe it took so long for us to reach lower Cedar.

I am a sucker for huckleberries and I never had any like these ones before. They were so large, cold and crisp and the greatest flavor that my taste buds would have experienced all day, but not even being close to what extraordinary view my eyes would see later that day.

When we arrived at lower Cedar, there was no time to take a detour and explore the lake, so we continued towards upper Cedar Lake. The more we increased in elevation, the more beautiful it got and by the time we stumbled upon upper Cedar, we knew we had to take a look around. The lake was so cold and clear and the location of it made it all the more incredible.

Surrounded by trees, tall cliffs, and the sun shining directly on it, the lake was postcard worthy. We eventually were able to free ourselves from the grasp that upper Cedar had on our senses and made our way up towards Dome Mountain. However, the beauty of the great outdoors continued to seize us. There was nothing like the view of being able to see both lakes side by side and the vast landscape beyond them. However, unable to stop time, we were forced to keep walking.

Once we were behind the mountain, we were able to take a lunch break in a little meadow that contained something that seemed almost like magic. "Flying spiders" were all around the meadow and even though they were "flying" from the support of their webs, the way they appeared in the sun was captivating.

After lunch, we continued our trek towards Dome. As we began to approach closer to our destination, we were facing the largest rockslide I had ever seen. Seeing as if it was the easiest route, we were able to reach the valley located between Dome and its "partner." Once we reached the top, we were greeted with the most magnificent view and the famous jar that enabled us to leave our names as proof of our accomplishment. This was the icing on top of the cake.

I really never knew where I lived until I was looking at all the mountains and bodies of water that surrounded Libby. Since that day up on Dome Mountain, I have never taken this little town for granted. Libby isn't merely what asbestos has portrayed it to be, it is one of the most gorgeous places on earth. This is why Dome Mountain is my most memorable wilderness experience. It helped me fall in love with my hometown and to appreciate what the wilderness has to offer.

voices in the
wilderness

Callahan Peel was the winner of the 2015 Friends of Scotchman Peaks Wilderness scholarship essay competition for Troy High School. Her story appeared in *The Western News* in the June 30, 2015 edition.

time on the water

Throughout my life, I have spent an immeasurable
amount of time on the water. I live a few miles from Bull Lake, and my
house is about 200 yards from Lake Creek. My dad worked as a raft guide
for many years, and he took me rafting on many occasions. You wouldn't
think, then, that a tiny little creek in the Kootenai National Forest would
best me. Allow me to back up and tell the full story.

The day was shaping up to be a scorcher in late July 2012. It was around
90 degrees out, and had not rained in weeks. I was relaxing with three
friends in Libby between sessions of soccer camp. We needed to pass the
time between practices and it had to involve something to cool us down.

One friend suggested that we should go to the lake, but it was unap-
pealing, as we had already done that. Another mentioned hiking, but the
idea was quickly shot down when we all thought about the heat. After an
hour of bickering, a teammate suggested that we float a river about ten
miles outside of Libby.

We only had a couple of hours until our next session of soccer, so we set to work rounding up life jackets, floaties, and food. We dropped one car off at our exit point and all piled into one car, unloading at our starting point. Ditching our shoes and phones, we blew up our floaties and hopped into the river.

At first, the trip was carefree. With our toes in the cool water, it no longer felt like the sun was causing heat stroke. The sky was a gorgeous blue, the trees were a luscious green, and it smelled perfect. The smell you only experience when it is a hot summer day and you are in the forest. Overall, the day was shaping up to be one of those perfect summer days.

That is, until the first time our floaties grounded. It was not a big deal; we just picked up the floaties and food, walked a couple of yards, and plunked back in where the water was deeper. We started floating again and soon, I was back to feeling warm and content. Then we grounded again. And again. And again. With each grounding, our float time was reduced until we were not floating so much as walking through a dry creek bed. The creek was reduced to a trickle of a stream and we decided it was time to stop and troubleshoot. We were probably two miles from the car, stuck barefoot with no phones, no shoes, but enough food to feed a small settlement of people.

We had three options. We could hike back to our cars, hike out to our friend's house, or attempt to build a homestead right there in the creek bed, where we would survive off of our huge amount of food. Obviously, the last option was not ideal, and it ended up having to come to a vote. Looking back, we did not choose the easiest option: hiking back to the car. We were only a few miles away, and it would have taken us less than an hour.

Instead, we decided to hike out to our friend's house, without knowledge of the exact location, or the distance of which we would have to traverse barefoot. We packed up our gear, and were ready to go, until we realized we could not carry all of the food. With no other options, we ate all of the food, piled the trash into one bag, and carried it out. We were then four barefoot, tired, sunburnt, and extremely full teenagers. We hiked and hiked. I got many scrapes and cuts from hiking through the underbrush, and a few of them turned into lasting scars.

We hiked through the trees, where the foliage was so thick that the sun was blocked and we became cold as well. We hiked a couple more hours and eventually we reached a paved road. I cried with relief. Eventually we reached the house. I promptly collapsed on a couch with relief. We all started cracking jokes and talked about what an incredible day it was. Despite the scrapes, bruises, sunburns, abused feet and the fact that we missed the evening camp session, it really was one of those amazing summer days. We were surrounded by nature, and were amongst good companies. That, in the end, is all that really matters.

voices in the
wilderness

Pat McLeod and her husband Charlie grew up in Lincoln County. They have returned to their roots after nearly three decades away from home.

trail work as a healing experience

When I read about an overnight work detail in the Friends Of Scotchman Peaks Wilderness Newsletter, I hesitated before signing up for. Questions in my mind included: Was I physically strong enough to do trail maintenance? Would I be able to set up the tent alone? Who would I be camping with?

However, the lure of a night in the mountains gave me courage to sign up. After all, I had spent the last few years in my Houston office, looking at a picture on the wall of the Cabinet Mountains Wilderness and dreaming of retirement when I could hike. And my husband Charlie had even given me a new tent as a retirement gift that had not yet been on a backpacking trip.

I was born and raised in Libby and Troy, and it was Charlie — who graduated from Troy High School — who introduced me to the joy of hiking. After graduating from

voices in the
wilderness

Montana State University, we moved to Houston, but returned home to Troy every
year and usually took a summer backpacking trip. Hiking in the Kootenai National
Forest was a way to detox; a time when the only human sound I heard was my own
heart and with each hard breath I replaced the traffic clogged city air with pure cool
mountain freshness. At the end of a hike, I was exhausted but also recharged.

Soon after retirement, I was spending my summer in Montana. I was doing
day hikes, and a freak accident on the Little Spar Trail — a rock fell on my leg
and broke it — caused me to be carried off the mountain by David Thompson
Search and Rescue. I was in St John's Hospital for a week and spent many months
on crutches. My recovery took more than a year, during which time my dreams
of sleeping in the Cabinet Mountain Wilderness had to wait.

When I read about the trail project in *Peak Experience*, I had been working
hard to regained strength and stamina. Was I ready to volunteer? There was one
way to find out. I signed up for trail maintenance.

At the appointed time, we volunteers gathered at the trailhead where we met
Forest Service staff who issued me a pair of loppers. The weather was ideal and
the conversation enjoyable as we started up the trail. Still the question remained,
could I keep up? All worked out great because when I needed to rest, I stopped
and trimmed some vegetation along the trail.

I did it!!! I made it to the campsite. It was a personal accomplishment of great
significance after more than a year of recovery. And, the campsite was in a fabu-
lous spot overlooking the Bull River Valley.

My biggest contribution to the group experience may have been bringing
Jumbo marshmallows for roasting over the campfire. The s'mores were great
but even better was seeing my fellow campers with marshmallow all over their
face and hands. It was a joyful evening of staring into the campfire and listening
to trail tails. We were no longer just a group of volunteers, we now knew more
about each other and friendships were being established.

All of my previous backpacking had been with my husband and he had put up the tent. However, he was not yet retired. On this trip, I was on my own. For the first time ever, I found my own camp spot and set up the tent. It was not too long after attempting to fall asleep that I discovered the importance of flat ground. A slight incline meant I was sliding against the side of the tent all night. Oh, well. After a successful day, it was not hard to fall asleep.

Going with the group of experienced backpacker was great. Sandy Compton expertly hung our packs in a tree following all bear safety rules.

The next morning serious, hard work with the Pulaski was in full swing as we began cutting trail. With new self-confidence and a quick lesson, I too was swinging a Pulaski. What pride I felt. I was part of a group that was contributing to the stewardship of our National Forest.

voices in the
wilderness

Shey Hannum was the 2016 winner of the Friends of Scotchman Peaks Wilderness scholarship essay contest for Thompson Falls High School. Her essay appeared in the *Sanders County Ledger* in September of 2016.

calling in the big one

I bet you've never heard a hunting story like the one
I'm about to tell you; especially from a girl. This is the craziest hunting experience that I've ever had, along with being one I'll never forget. Even though it might be hard to seem real, all the things that happened are true.

Beep! Beep! Beep! My alarm went off at 5:00am. I jumped out of bed already excited that I was going hunting with my dad. I ran upstairs to wake him up. Within twenty minutes we both got ready and piled into the truck. I asked where we were going today and dad said I got to pick. I picked a place that we hadn't gone yet this season. We talked on the drive up the mountain and occasionally would stop to bugle, seeing if a bull would answer. A couple did, but they were pretty far off. We kept driving.

Sometime later, we stopped and I bugled. A big bull responded, not too far off too! My dad grabbed his bow and pack, and we went off to find the big guy. After a while we stopped and I bugled again. The bull responded. Suddenly, my dad froze and put his hand back in signal for me to do the same. Very slowly I looked around; we had come upon the bull's cows. There were probably twenty feeding above and ahead of us. One cow in particular had spotted our movement and was bobbing her head to see what we were. She started trotting away and every so often looked back in our direction. The other cows knew something was up and in no time were all running over to the other side of the mountain.

Sighing, my dad told me that we wouldn't be able to catch them since they were spooked. He said that we could try to go further up and maybe catch something on the other side.

We trekked up for a good hour and a half, by that

time I was famished. We stopped on the side of the mountain where we had the whole view of the valley. It was so breathtaking! Dad took out our sandwiches and we sat on that hillside in silence just appreciating the scenery. It was then that I thought 'It doesn't get much better than this.' While finishing up our PB&Honeys, I kept thinking about how lucky I was to live here in Montana.

Once again we set off up the mountain. I bugled and a huge bull answered, very close. I told dad that if he went and sat ahead of me a ways that I'd bugle him in so he could get a shot. He crept about 20 yards out in front of me. I bugled once and the bull screamed back at me. I got chills and smiled at the same time because he was so close. Dad pulled back his bow. I grunted into the bugle and at that, he came into sight.

He was beautiful, so huge! I heard him breathing and I held my breath so he wouldn't hear me. Dad shot and the bull took off. I stood up with the biggest smile on my face as I looked at dad. "I missed" he said and my face fell. We checked for blood or hair and when we found the arrow, that confirmed the miss. We decided to head home.

On the way home, we found a road and followed it back to the direction of the truck. While we were walking, something moved under my boot. I screamed and saw that it was only a Gardner Snake. He jokingly said "surprised you didn't call something in." I laughed and at that moment something crashed in the brush above the bank. A bloodcurdling cry rang out and I jumped behind my dad, panicked! A mountain lion had attacked a deer! I was freaked out and my dad pulled out his pistol. For a few seconds we just stared at each other and then just as stealthily as it had come, the cat disappeared.

Safe to say we booked it out of there in a hurry. Although we didn't get anything that day, I will never forget that amazing experience. Seeing a cat attack a deer is not something you see every day, not to mention seeing a 7x7 bull either! This is definitely one of the most memorable wilderness experiences that I've ever had.

voices in the
wilderness

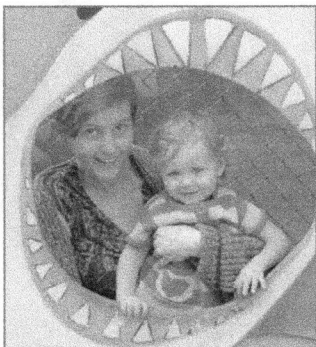

Kristina Boyd works for the
Yaak Valley Forest Council. Her daughter is
now learning to play the harmonica, most
assuredly so she will know an instrument
that will fit in a backpack.

Kristina
Boyd

adding to the pack

For over a thousand nights, I had slept in the same
position in my beloved mummy bag: left forearm squashed between my
belly and the ground, right hand cushioning my head, left leg straight
down and right leg tucked up almost to my chin. Thirteen springs, summers and falls had seen me working in the woods in all types of wild
places and sleeping wherever it made sense that week. There was no other
way I would have preferred to spend my time than roaming in the wild.

For six of those years I tracked and radio-collared wolves throughout
northwest Montana. It was one of my most independent and nomadic
positions. But during my last field season, a couple of summers ago now,
I brought a tag-along with me. And one night as I shimmied into position in my familiar way, my belly decided that it could no longer abide
that trusty sleeping contortion.

Pregnancy, and all of the domesticity it implies, can be an unnerving
rite of passage for women who are born with the wind in their veins and

pine boughs as their bower. But finding a new ground sleeping position? Now that was really getting personal. I lay on my back and listened to the evening, trying to quiet my mind. The flute of a Swainson's thrush came first, rising like a leaf in the breeze. Then a northern waterthrush skipped his song out like a pebble over a pool. A waft of pine passed through my tent, my daughter pressed some appendage against my ribs, and I felt peace. Sleep steamrolled over my discomfort, as it usually does after a long day in the outdoors.

There is a lot of hiking involved in tracking wolves; on beautiful trails and those that have seen better days; on knapweed-smothered roads and those that brought me to my knees to cruise the alder like, well… a dog; and on the untamed forest floor getting from points A to B in the shortest distance but inevitably the longest time. And there is an awful lot of driving on rocky forest roads. An awful lot. Before and after every hike, during each trapline set and check, and in the evenings over boxed instant whatnots with a splash of hot sauce added for pizazz, my colleagues would check in with me. Were my ankles swollen? Did I need more food? Was I over-tired? Yes. But if they had asked me if I was on cloud nine, my answer would have been the same.

With fresh air and a pumping heart elevating my thoughts, my hikes were occasions to share feel-good endorphin boosts with my daughter, rather than the stew of trepidation and frustration that sitting at home tended to simmer up. And the cadence of my movement settled her better than any song. Even the long dawn and dusk trap-check drives seemed to soothe her with their jaunty rhythms.

But it was not all routine and humdrum. We had some pint-sized adventures together too. My favorite was the mama grouse who burst out of the alder like a shotgun and chased my waddling frame and screaming,

laughing banshee wail for fifty raucous yards. Another interlude, during a morning bicycle trap check up a steep closed road, was the moment
when my little joker decided it was a good time to finally flip head-down
and knock me off my bike in alarm. And then there were the rare times
when we stood motionless and took it all in as the penetrating howl of
wolves reverberated through our cores.

Two years have passed since that summer ended and
our shared rite of passage began: one that does not allow for much roaming in the wild. In my veins, I feel the stillness where the wind once ran.
My pine bower has been usurped by an oak rocking chair. I struggle with
envy toward those who have the time and energy to wander the woods.
But I also see touches of the wild in my daughter: the way that only a
swaying bounce would soothe her as an infant, her love of fear and effort
and log-walking, and the softly whispered "wow" that she utters at the
scents and sounds and sights of nature.

My husband and I took her camping for the first time just a few weeks
ago, on her second birthday. Even as she slept, tucked into her own tiny
sleeping bag, I could see phosphorescent traces of the light in her eyes
that had shone so brightly that day. I shimmied my way into my neglected
mummy bag and a surge of peace coursed through me. I turned over and
tucked my right hand under my left cheek, my left arm under my belly,
and my right knee up almost to my chin. We would do this again, many
times. The wild is waiting.

voices in the
wilderness

Ray Stout works for Rosauers
in Libby. He is also a writer and historian.

i'll be slammed

I don't know when I began to feel nervous, whether at the first gust of wind or crack of lightning. Or boom of thunder. Maybe when the afternoon turned dark. I don't even remember which came first.

I do remember hurtling down that trail. And hardly voluntarily. I flew, hoping I would make the next switchback in that stand of mature timber, of dense, falling, crashing trunks a foot or more thick.

Somehow, it seemed the very fury of a wildland scorned.

Those regal killers. I couldn't see the trees for the force — survival — driving me down that hill, what with the gale, rain, gloom, thunder, and flashes. The air up there was so violent, so dark, I couldn't trust my vision. I'd hear them topple to the ground, sometimes seconds between, sometimes their shattering simultaneous, the toys of a drunken deity playing dominoes. Whether onto the tread or into this solo hiker, I couldn't tell as the crackling of boles vied with the whoosh of the wind.

And all reason was out the window.

Wildness, supposedly, helps keep the world alive. But in wild storms was not necessarily the preservation of the individual.

What hit me so hard was how I careened out of that Needles Roadless Area in central Idaho. So knee-jerk, so instinctive. I might have met head-on one of those falling giants, its plummeting top invisible up there in the canopy. Ditto had I halted. Slammed if I do, slammed if I don't. Somehow, mind was the lesser as body chose between the equal of two evils: I just ran, like a wound-up toy.

Twenty-two years later, the lightning has struck me.

The concussion rings with a contrast: of the beautiful side of *wild* with the fearsome. And it reverberates. With more contrast. Not just in the obvious ways — safety versus jeopardy, risk with reward, take your bad with your good, and so on — but in deeper.

It's penetrated the wilderness that is part of my quintessence. That inner landscape has certainly been shaped by storms of emotion as well as spells of serenity. And what that tempest did, I realize, is unravel a more crucial part of that essence: that there is such a thing as peace and sanctuary.

For all I know I could've been born into some world where any contentment is inconceivable. Unthinkable. But here there can be, for example, goodwill as opposed to animosity. Quenchedness against thirst. A cathedral of (motionless) old-growth cedars dwarfing their litter, duff and humus versus a slum full of littered hummus cartons.

I may not always have the good things, but I know they're there and worth running for. And that my mind is capable of choosing to, usually. The world I know is not, for the most part, a place of constant agitation or peril.

I reached the wet, windy gravel road, relieved to at least be off that narrow footpath. Such an eerie, charged atmosphere. I scurried back to the guard station, unnerved, unscathed, and in the dark about what an electrical transformer I had just passed through.

What hits me so hard is how I saunter into this novel boundless area in central essence, not a spooked saddle horse but at the mind's rule, feeling much more confident I'll get there. And if something hits me en route, I'll make what good I can of it.

I guess it took one long, lingering flash of lightning to make me see the light.

Well, I'll be slammed.

*After the storm. Blowdown near Star Peak
Trail #999 in the Scotchman Peaks.*

voices in the
wilderness

Jason Martin Schnackenberg
of Libby submitted this piece as his entry
into the 2014 Friends of Scotchman Peaks
Wilderness essay scholarship contest.

Jason
Schnackenberg

baptizing zach

I have had many experiences in the outdoors that have left tremendous impacts on my life and have continually cultivated in me a deep passion for the outdoors. However, my most memorable experience, the one that I will absolutely never forget, occurred last summer when I had the opportunity to hike to Crater Lake, which lies in a basin just below the Peak of Treasure Mountain in the Cabinet Mountain range. I was accompanied by a group of five other great guys, who were all just as excited for the hike up to the lake as I was.

We were all looking forward to the hike, but this was only part of the reason we were so excited for the day. Two of the guys in our group, Tatum and Zach Haines, were father and son, and what made this experience so special and unique is that we were hiking specifically to Crater Lake so that Tatum and Zach could get baptized. It was Tatum and Zach's goal to be baptized in a place they would never forget, and what a place it was.

What makes this story even more amazing is that Zach Hanes was only 11 years old and battling a terribly aggressive bout of brain cancer when we made this hike. He had just recently recovered enough of his strength, that he had lost from Chemotherapy treatments, to be able to attempt the 4500 vertical foot climb.

We got up early on a beautiful Saturday morning and met up at the bottom of the mountain where our starting point for the hike was. The trek to Crater Lake is usually expected to be a six to seven hour hike when it is hiked at a strong steady pace. Due to Zach's health issues, we were expecting the hike to be a little bit longer, around eight or nine hours. With this in mind, we started up the mountain early enough so that we could make it back before dark.

The first legs of the hike were not too rough because we had a nice trail to follow, but as we continued, the trail eventually dissipated into various small game trails until finally we were bush whacking through extremely thick forest and trudging along at a very slow pace. The entire time up the mountain, we would stop every ten minutes or so to allow Zach time to rest and recuperate. He could only keep going for small stretches before he would get winded and need a break. Through the grueling hike, Zach continued until we finally reached the lake, at a much later time than expected, but it was well worth the effort. Tatum got baptized by another from our group and soon after, baptized his son, Zach. Seeing the joy on their faces when they came up out of the water was an amazing experience.

After they were baptized, we spent some more time at the lake, jumping in the water to get refreshed and just enjoying the beautiful scenery. As the time came to head back down, we did so with happy hearts. Zach continued to be strong the entire way down, even when it started getting dark, until we finally reached the trucks, twelve hours after we had left. Taking much longer than we originally intended, and hiking the terrain that we did, Zach proved how strong he was. Being able to witness his baptism in such a beautiful and awe inspiring environment was one of the greatest privileges I have ever had. Seeing his determination to complete this hike was an inspiration. After that amazing day, Zach Haines courageously continued his battle with cancer for the next five months until he left for his true home on January 18, 2014, at age 11.

Sandy Compton photo

Snowshoe Lake in the Cabinet Mountains Wilderness.

Sarah McBride graduated from Libby High School. She participated in the Kootenai Outdoor Adventure Program (KOAP) as a sixth grader, and was a counselor with KOAP during the summer before her senior year.

Sara
McBride

the only way to live

I remember looking out and thinking to myself, "Wow, I can see the whole world from here. . . " That moment, the moment on the mountaintop, changed my life. From that point on, I knew I NEEDED to be outdoors.

I grew up in the middle of nowhere, which meant living among the trees. But, I didn't appreciate the world around me. I did everything in my power to stay indoors, even volunteering to do chores. I look back with my outdoor-loving eyes, and realize how foolish I was. I mean, I went outside, but didn't love every minute of it. My family enjoyed time outdoors, but it wasn't by my choice. It wasn't until that moment.

I was in sixth grade, and very scared to try new things. But I took a leap of faith and decided to join a thing called the K.O.A.P.* I had no idea what it stood for, but I knew you hiked in this "thing." I signed up, and was accepted. Come to find out, it was backpacking too, not just day hikes. I was terrified! Not loving the outdoors, and now, jumping into it. The first hike came, and it was fine. I was shocked by this realization. Then the next one, and the next, and the rest of them — until the backpacking trip. I was beginning to truly see what the world around me had to offer; done being foolish, and able to see what I had been missing out on.

Now came time for *the* trip.

We left early in the morning after spending the previous day packing. My anticipation and anxiety grew as the sight of civilization fled from view. We arrived at the trailhead, seeing nothing but trees. This made me nervous. How was I supposed to have fun with nothing around me. And then we hiked, hearing nothing but the birds singing their soulful songs, and the slight breeze stirring leaves. The air was crisp. This was unfamiliar territory. I thought this was the best thing I had ever experienced. I thought this several times throughout the trip.

On our second-to-last day, we moved locations of camp, having to hike a distance. Again, we woke up early to pack up and move out. We had been hiking what seemed to be a ninety-degree angle for about three hours. We reached the peak, and one by one, we climbed to the very top. In that moment, when I reached the summit, I felt like I was finally introduced to what the world is suppose to be: breathless.

Every hair on my body stood up, and I was frozen in my spot. I was on top of the world. Below me, I saw my previous way of life, so small and meaningless. But on top of this mountain I saw my future. The sky was bluer, trees greener and life easier. I wanted to feel invincible forever. I knew, in that moment, on that mountaintop whose name I never knew, being in the outdoors was the only way to live.

The rest of the trip, I was probably the obnoxious one; pointing out the color of the moss on the tall tree, or stopping in the middle of the trail to breathe the freshest air I could never imagine living without. All these new moments I never stopped to notice before.

Sadly, we came back to civilization, and away from the new love I had discovered. Returning home, I vowed to spend as little time inside as I could stand. And I have stayed true to this vow. I hike, backpack, kayak, camp, cross-country ski and do anything I can to be outside. Every time I walk out my front door now, I see how lucky I am to see natural beauty everywhere I look.

Kootenai Outdoor Adventure Project is an outdoor education program of Libby Public Schools.

voices in the
wilderness

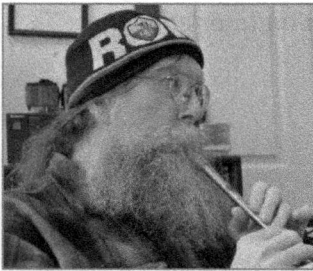

Brian Sherry, when he's not working as the volunteer program director at KVRZ public radio in Libby, sells antiques and collectibles at Left Hand Antiques.

Brian
Sherry

close encounters
of the moose kind

About 25 years ago, I took a couple weeks off from
work and went to Grand Teton National Park, which I had briefly visited
a few years earlier I wanted to do a little hiking and take some photos,
nothing out of the ordinary.

Earlier in the summer, I had hurt my knee playing softball, so nothing strenuous was planned, just easy day hikes. One of the hikes was a 3
mile loop that began and ended at the Jackson Lake Visitor Center. It was
a ideal hike, mostly flat with the loop starting about a half mile down the
trail. I chose to go by the pond, then loop around to the lake and back. At
the pond, there were some deer on the other side, so I stopped to watch
them through binoculars. Above me I heard bird call, and I looked up in

time to see an osprey with a fish being attacked by a bald eagle. I reached for my camera, and the osprey decided to drop the fish and fly off. The fish landed about 20 yards from me in the pond. It was still alive, barely, flopping every few minutes, with its tail in the water. With camera in hand, I waited for either bird to come back for the fish, and give me a perfect photo opportunity. It didn't happen, so sadly I moved on down the trail toward the lake.

The trail followed the lakeshore. I spotted a moose with a calf in the shallow water. Other hikers passed by with no problems, so I continued on down the trail, passing by with the moose, which were about 40 feet out in the water. Though I tried to not make much noise, the calf was disturbed by my presence, and he did a false charge (fortunately), which caused me to run back to where I had first spotted them. A couple of other hikers were at that spot, and, of course, one snidely asked: "What you doing — bugging the moose?"

After chatting with me a bit, they decided to take a chance, and got by the moose fine. So did a few hikers who followed. However, my knee was sore after sprinting away. I decided safety comes first, and that backtracking was the way to go.

I returned to where the loop joined the trail back to the visitors center, and then suddenly heard a crashing off to my immediate right. Much to my chagrin, there were those two moose running full speed, perpendicular to the trail, and right at me. Fortunately, they crossed the trail about 10 yards in front of me. However, after they passed, I heard nothing. There was no crashing sounds fading away as they ran off to my left. No snorting. Nothing. Just quiet.

This made me suspect they were lying in wait, ready to spook me again. I know from reading that's not in their nature, but after two close calls, I had to know if those were the moose from the lake. I turned around again and took the loop back around the pond and to the lake, where I saw no moose. Then, I continued on the trail by the lake and cautiously passed where they had crossed in front of me and made it back to the visitors center without any other problems.

After all this, in which I was charged while others could pass with no problems, and them running full speed through the woods, and hearing other moose stories, I've come to one conclusion: Moose are the drama queens of the wild!

voices in the
wilderness

Gunner Jordan wrote this essay for the 2013 Friends of Scotchman Peaks scholarship essay competition. He graduated from Troy High School in 2013.

let loose and discover yourself

I had never felt so at peace in my life than I did on the top of Grouse Ridge. A fall fog settled down below me, with the appearance of a lake covering all of the land. The sun had just begun to peek over the tops of the mountains east of me. All around me, of all sorts of different species of birds began chirping their little beaks off. It was such an amazing feeling, sitting atop the mountain alone — just me, the woodland creatures and the beautiful view of Montana's land.

I remember thinking to myself how crazy it would be if a mountain lion, a bear or something else showed up. Moments later, about twenty yards away from me, off to my left, a moose pushed his way through the thick brush and into the clearing where I resided. At first I was startled, but then the moose noticed me. Rather than trotting off or getting spooked, he just looked right at me and then began to sniff towards the ground. I wasn't sure what exactly the bull had been doing, but I knew he didn't find me a threat, so there was nothing to worry about.

By this time, the sun's heat had finally started getting intense. I shed a couple layers of my clothing and sat on a nearby log overlooking the lake of fog. I pulled out a sandwich I had prepared myself before I went on my journey.

There is no place like the peaceful woods to just pause life and truly enjoy the gift that we all have living in an area like Montana. The wild is a place where you can escape the reality of electronics, politics and school and just think — not particularly about one thing, but about everything; one subject or many. Alone out in the woods is by far the most spectacular place to just let loose and discover yourself.

After what seemed to have been hours of my day, but was actually just one, I decided that it was time for me to say goodbye to the woodland creatures and head back home. One of my homes anyway, for I consider the outdoors my home as well since it gives me a true sense of belonging, security, and comfort. I feel truly blessed to live in such a great place with so much wildlife and outdoor opportunities.

Stonebridge Ridge leads to Melissa Basin in the
proposed Scotchman Peaks Wilderness.

voices in the
wilderness

Makayla Cichosz-King's essay was the best from Libby High School in the 2013 Friends of Scotchman Peaks Wilderness scholarship competition.

Makayla
Cichosz-King

a ride on the wild side

I was very small when my grandparents took me to a horse ranch in the middle of nowhere. I had always loved horses, even if I was terrified of them and their big teeth. A lady greeted us as we climbed out of the car, and while the adults talked I awed at the dozens of horses surrounding me in their different corrals. My grandfather then departed to go fishing, and the lady brought out a horse for my grandmother and a pony for me.

His name was Little Joe, though I didn't see the irony in the name, seeing as he towered over me (and I had for years towered over my class-mates). The first moments on Little Joe's back were terrifying. My sneakers slipped in the stirrups, the heavy flanks rocked back and forth, and every so often the pony would canter to the side as if to throw me off, or toss his head as if to bite through my apple-sized knee.

Fortunately, my fear did not last long. My grandmother mounted her horse and the lady hers, and as she led us into the wilderness, I grew accustomed to the swaying of my pony and the lack of a safety belt. We just seemed to becoming fond of one another - with him eating at every slow moment and I gently berating him for it - when we descended a wooded hill behind my grandmother, and Little Joe's steady step failed him.

A log hidden in vegetation caught his hoof, I was later told, but all I knew at that moment was the drop of the pony's thick weight beneath me and my sudden airborne descent down the hill. In land covered in trees and sharp rocks and thorny bushes, the result could have been disastrous and easily fatal for one of us. However, I landed on soft ground covered in leaves, receiving minimal damage, and more miraculously, the lady was able to coax Little Joe to his shaky feet and ascertained that he had received no injury. Indeed, after our initial scare, we were both back to normal and quite eager to continue on. What's more, our fall and recovery seemed to strengthen the tenuous bond between us.

The lady led us up and down the wilderness for miles, and while she seemed to have difficulties with her own mount, Little Joe and I read each other perfectly. When she could not entice her horse into navigating a steep hill, Little Joe climbed it steadily. When she could not even pull her horse across a little bridge, I led Little Joe cantering gracefully across it. When she could not slow her horse to her command, I sped on Little Joe and bid him go faster until I was warned to stop. I did not want to, for I was feeling like the queen of the world on my pony, a daring racer and adventurer in a wild part of the world.

And at last, when we returned to the ranch, I begged for another ride. When my grandfather returned for us, I begged that he and my grandmother bring me back another day. I received vague promises, and as I sat in the back of the car, I worked hard to commit every moment to perfect memory. I watched Little Joe, tethered to a post, waiting to return to his corral, and I was convinced that, when I returned, he would remember me.

Sandy Compton photo

Pilik Ridge Trail #1036 is one of several
stock trails in the Scotchman Peaks.

voices in the
wilderness

Kaysha Hermann graduated
from Libby High School in 2016. She and
her classmate Trinity Wallace tied for best
overall essay in the 2016 Friends of Scotchman Peaks Wilderness scholarship essay
competition. Trinity's essay follows this.

Kaysha
Hermann

horse and chickadee

Cool, crisp air that seems to crunch between my teeth like that of a honeycrisp apple meets my enthralled senses as I clasp my horse's reins tight. The sharp tang of pine and the soft mixture of larch mixed with the cold makes a sort of ease come over me. Today is a good day for a ride, I thought. Nothing can match the feeling of adventure that courses through my veins in a rapid pulse right now. Plus, the silent lack of judgment emanating from my horse makes all the troubles of the day seem to slip away.

Herdalgo, as if hearing my thoughts, turns her head to look at me imploringly as if saying, "Why must you take so long? We have a trail to follow behind Kenny's house, down Hammerhead Cut-Off, and it's getting dark."

I laugh and place my foot in the crook of the stirrups. With a loud grunt, I lift and swing my other leg over the long expanse of my horse's back. The crackle of leather shifts under me as I adjust my weight comfortably. While I do this, the rough texture of the reins meets my hands in a familiar way that makes a smile meet my lips, as my horse sidesteps underneath me. Sun slants through all the while, creating a dappled effect on the back of my paint mare and me. I revel in this warmth coming through in the rare times it does on such a winter day as this, and I almost want to curl up in a tight ball like that of a simple house cat. I shake myself and urge my horse forward with the clicking of my tongue and slight pressure on her rib cage. She blusters, her breath stirring a white cloud into the air, and reluctantly steps forward.

The mountain ahead of us is stark compared to the drab grey of the sky and inspires a sense of awe within me as we slowly stumble our way up the sinuous trail. Cracking twigs snap beneath us and an infrequent, oddly-placed bird flits to each branch above us, trilling its lonely tune. I can almost imagine all the animals tucked away for the winter except for this bird. I glance up wonderingly at it as it flies by again and nod my head in confirmation of the chickadee's grey-brown dusted chest. We are alike after all.

The bird with its hopeful expectations and straightforward path is mutually met with mine. We both love the mystery of the trail, and we will always remember this day as a day when cognitive thoughts intermingled with the hard, packed earth, the trees and every semblance of life within these towering mountains. So for once, both me and the chickadee, fall into the humble awe of our small stature.

horse and
chickadee

Trinity Wallace was co-winner of the Friends of Scotchman Peaks Wilderness Scholarship Essay competition for 2016. She shared the honors with her Libby High School classmate Kaysha Hermann.

Trinity
Wallace

finding the bigger picture

I have always been captivated by nature; nature has a way of making my first-world problems seem little compared to the vast majority of the world. Any chance I get I am out and about exploring and finding new places to adventure. It is hard for me to pick my favorite experience, because all of them have been very influential in shaping how I see the world today, but I can narrow it down to the time I hiked into a secluded mountain lake with my family this past summer.

Little Spar Lake is a four-mile hike deep in grizzly country. The wild-life and scenery are breathtaking, with the trail crossing over creeks and winding through the forest. When the trail opens up to reveal the crystal blue waters nestled in the middle of nowhere, it gives one the feeling of vastness and peace. The lake and shale rocks that line it are untouched by man which gave my family the perfect opportunity to unplug from every-day life and truly appreciate all that our part of the country possesses. I want my little sister and generations after her to have the opportunity to witness this beauty and help preserve it for others as well.

When the lake first came into view, I remember the feeling I had. It was as if someone had taken the air from my lungs. In that moment I was taken back from all the complex norms of society today. I was left speechless in the presence of such vast simplicity. I continued my journey to the edge of the lake, through the tall rice grass and over the rough rocks. When I arrived at the water's edge I sat upon a large, protruding rock that allowed me to sit suspended over the water. Sitting on this perfectly placed rock, I was taken to a place where my thoughts could roam free. Sitting under the vast, blue sky I felt small compared the tremendous amount of space that encompassed me. I remember how differently I looked at things.

I was not critical of the lake's elegance. I was appreciative. But more than that I was worried. I was worried that later generations would not have the opportunity to experience such eye opening beauty that the world presents for us. I worry that we take this world for granted. We as humans use things so cheaply, with the feeling that everything can be replaced. We cannot replace what we destroy in nature, and I fear that one day we will live with the feeling of guilt and regret for our actions.

As I sat upon this rock, with all this roving around my mind, I couldn't shake the feeling of hope. Although I was worrisome for the future, I was also hopeful. I have hope that society can change our conventional ways. The idea that one can be happy without all of these extra luxuries has been stuck in my mind since that day. This thought has affected the way I want to spend my future and how I will dedicate my time. On my walk back to my family's vehicle, I felt like a different person. I felt more understanding of the things around me, but I also wanted to make a stand. I want to show people that you do not need technology to see the bigger picture because the bigger picture is right in front of all of us, if only one opens the window.

The big picture from the big rock at Litte Spar Lake in the proposed Scotchman Peaks Wilderness

www.ingramcontent.com/pod-product-compliance
Lightning Source LLC
Chambersburg PA
CBHW060501280326
41933CB00014B/2821